To
My lovel...
with love from
Stella

HELD HOSTAGE TO A DISEASE

WHY ME GOD?

MARGARET CORNELL

FOREWORD
DAN CHESNEY

Published by
Maurice Wylie Media
Inspirational Christian Publisher

Publishers' statement: Throughout this book the love for our God is such that whenever we refer to Him, we honour with Capitals. On the other hand, when referring to the devil, we refuse to acknowledge him with any honour to the point of violating grammatical rule and withholding capitalisation.

For more information visit
www.MauriceWylieMedia.com

Endorsements

"When I think of Tony and Margaret Cornell the word that leaps to mind is faith. Even in the darkest days of Margaret's cancer treatment I never met with them without my faith being boosted. This book has precisely the same effect. If you are contending for a healing miracle or need your faith encouraged, this book is an absolute must. Maybe you have doubts about healing; suspend your judgement until you have finished this." (Hebrews 11:6)

Daniel Holland, Evangelist with "Through Faith Missions."

"Please pick up a copy of Margaret's testimony of healing. It will bless you and encourage you for your own healing."

Ash Kotecha, Healing Evangelist.

"First of all, I'd like to say that I've known Margaret and Tony Cornell for over 30 years, having met them early in my coming to England. I had the honour of speaking at their church in Ely, Cambs, several times over the years, stayed in their large home where they took in people in need, discipling them and caring for them completely unselfishly. They are both true Christians; followers of Jesus with tons of works to validate it.

Because of my intimate knowledge of their complete integrity and deep faith in preaching and teaching the gospel in the power of its truth, and knowing first hand of their depth of love for people, it was truly my pleasure to read Margaret's testimonial of her triumphs and trials in her bout of sickness.

I love her deep transparency of the ups and downs of her battle, and the sheer honesty of her heart in sharing how her faith in Christ brought her through, and her heartfelt desire to believe in what she knew to be God's truth.

Sincerely her book will bolster any who are battling illness and strengthen their desire to fully surrender to the faithfulness of Jesus to do what he always did; heal the sick.

Her writing is honest, filled with wonderful humour, and casual in its offering, making it an easy read, and a tool of strength. I guarantee that you will be encouraged and blessed, as you read her story."

Rod Anderson, Senior Pastor. Commonwealth Christian Fellowship, London.

"A story of inspiration of one woman's faith, as she overcame stage four Lymphoma. Hear the steps the Lord told her to follow to obtain victory."

Dr. Mark Virkler, Communion with God Ministries.

"As a fellow believer who has lived by faith for many years, I can say that this book will be a breath of fresh air, because not only will you be strengthened in your faith, but you will hear how honesty is need when stepping out in faith. Margaret faced her sickness not with presumptuous confessions but with wisdom. As Jesus told us we are to weigh up our situation before we make our decision, and that is what Margaret did. She understood the consequences if Jesus did not heal her. Margaret faced the fact that God is either her healer or He is not and, knowing the possibility that she could die, she decided to believe God anyway.

Faith always costs; Margaret faced that cost and came up believing, Margaret proved that God is who He says He is and that He does what He says He will do. Now that is real living; and I hope that all who read this book will be inspired to step out in real faith in the God who never fails."

Dan Chesney. Pastor of London Alive Church and LG3 Ministries, England.

"This is more than a testimony of walking with Jesus from cancer to health – it is a comprehensive manual on keeping and enjoying abundant life. This will be a helpful book for many people."

Dr. Barrie Lawrence, Chairman of the National Council of the Full Gospel Businessmen, UK & Ireland.

A special word from a friend...

"Walking alongside my dear friend Margaret through this trial has been an absolute privilege. She is one of the most loving, faith-filled people you could ever meet. This honest account of her journey, truly reflects her deep relationship with the Father, always believing that God is good.

Seeing Margaret so poorly during and after the chemotherapy was so very hard, and I would often have to pull myself back and remember the promises over my friend's life.

Over the years she has built up an overflowing storehouse of God's word in her heart and it was an absolute joy to read healing scriptures with her during the many hours I sat by her side.

There were often tears, but always followed by joy and laughter. I should also document that flat whites and pavlovas were also a part of her healing process!

This lady is so inspirational, and I will be forever grateful for all that she has taught me. I pray that this book will inspire others in their journey, both for themselves and for others that they care for."

Claire Denniss, Isleham, England.

Dedication

To my dear Lord and Saviour Jesus Christ,
my husband Tony; our children Ben and Giles
and our 4 wonderful grandchildren.
To all the precious people who
so diligently supported me
during a such time of great trial.

Contents

Appendix

Foreword

As a fellow believer who has lived by faith many years, I can say that this book will be a breath of fresh air, because not only will you be strengthened in your faith, but you will hear how honesty is needed when stepping out in faith.

Margaret faced her sickness, not with presumptuous confessions, but with wisdom. As Jesus told us, we are to weigh up our situation before we make our decision, and that is what Margaret did.

She understood the consequences if Jesus did not heal her.

She faced the fact that God is either her Healer or He is not.

And knowing the possibility that she could die, she decided to believe God anyway.

Faith always costs, and Margaret faced that cost and came up believing. Margaret proved that God is who He says He is and that He does what He says He will do. Now that is real living!

We would all like to see the results Margaret had in being healed or having our prayers answered in such a dynamic way, and when we don't, we wonder why. This book helps us with that enigma as she shares openly her relationship with God.

Notice how prayer, wisdom, humility, listening to the Holy Spirit and faith in God's word, all worked together to bring her to the fulfilment of the promise that Jesus Christ is our Healer.

I hope that all who read this book will be inspired to step out in real faith in the God who never fails.

Dan Chesney. Pastor of London Alive Church and LG3 Ministries

Introduction

I felt compelled to write this book because I have seen so many Christians die or stay captive to sickness, particularly cancer; but what if there is a way of escape and they've just not found it?

Cancer now affects one in every two people. It's crouching at the door of many lives, so asking; "Why me, God?" could easily be changed to; "Why not me, God?"

Much of the church has either not believed that healing is for today because we now have science and medical treatment, or they have believed that sickness is God's way of teaching His children something. If we do not know our covenant or understand the power of the Word of God, we can only live just like those who do not know God, and at the mercy of all that the world, the flesh, the devil and the unbelieving church offer.

When faced with this life-threatening disease, I felt trapped, and taken hostage by an enemy I never believed I would have to face. Fortunately, I never believed that it had come from God and I knew that God heals today; but when they suggested I had two months to live without medical treatment, I knew that the chips were down! The big question was: would God heal me?

I had just one week of seeking the Lord to show me the path I should take to healing. It was not easy, but I brought all my questions to Him and found my answer.

It was a journey backed by knowing who I was in Him, and who He is in me and most importantly; how to hear His voice, more than my own or that of others.

What I have learnt over 30 plus years I have placed in this book, so
you too can enter that place of promise and walk out the victory of
God in your own life.

Margaret Cornell

CHAPTER 1

Will nobody believe me?

Despite looking well in August 2017, as we came into the month of September, I started to feel very ill. I felt so tired; unusually tired, especially for a person who loves life and is typically very energetic.

Within a few days, I realised that I had yet *another* urine infection, of which I'd had many in recent months, but it was so severe, it felt like my remaining kidney stones were trying to get out! The urology nurse arranged for me to have an x-ray which showed the tiny stones still firmly in place; and, reluctantly, I had more antibiotics for the infection. Then I began to have excruciating pains in my upper stomach area which kept me awake at night, and of course also kept my long-suffering husband Tony awake, night after night!

The pain was so very severe, I was sometimes rolling around on the bed, or walking about the house praying, unable to settle down and rest, even though I'd taken both paracetamol and codeine. This went on for two whole weeks!

It was awful. I hardly slept and I didn't want to eat because it felt like my stomach was already full, and I was losing a lot of weight. I just assumed that the pain and the lack of food was the reason I was losing weight. Just before this, at the end of the summer, after I had seen a photograph of myself at a church picnic lying on a rug… I had said to Tony; "*Goodness I look like a beached whale... we must go on a diet!*"

I never dreamed that I was just about to lose a massive amount of weight without trying! At one point during this period I had even gone to the Accident and Emergency department in my local hospital where I was scanned and told I had gall stones and given stronger pain killers.

In total, during this awful period of time I saw five different doctors and GP's. Eventually, one of the doctors, after I begged him to do so, sent me to hospital for further investigation.

It seems very odd, that although I told him that I was having terrible bouts of pain and had lost two and a half stone (35 lbs) and was having classic symptoms of the disease, with which I was eventually diagnosed; he was somewhat reluctant. He told me that the hospital would probably think he was being rather silly.

Perhaps I just sounded too calm, too matter of fact, to be taken seriously?

Much later, I had a telephone call from a doctor at my surgery apologising that none of them had picked up how ill I was.

Then came the good news and the bad!

I went to Addenbrookes hospital and was admitted. After I had a scan, I was told once again, that the pain was probably due to gallstones, and I was very glad that they gave me paracetamol, codeine and also morphine, which dulled the pain. I was greatly relieved. However, the next day a consultant came to me, stood in the room, and, shifting uncomfortably from one foot to the other, said; "*We think you have Lymphoma.*"

Utter disbelief filled my mind and I said: "*No, surely not... You mean cancer? Are you sure it couldn't be anything else?*" He calmly replied;

"Well… it could be an infection. but we don't think so. We think it's Lymphoma." I was staggered. It felt unreal.

He offered me a biopsy. When I caught sight of the screen out of the corner of my eye, I could see there were *'swellings'* and it obviously confirmed that I had something bad. A few days later I had a telephone call from a nurse at Addenbrookes giving me an appointment with an oncologist to see about the lymphoma.

"Ah" I said. *"So, it's definite is it?"* *"Didn't you know?"* she said. I took a deep breath and replied; *"Well… I sort of knew but it had not been officially confirmed."*

The nurse was absolutely horrified that she had informed me of such a serious diagnosis in such a casual way over the telephone. She thought that I already knew the results of the biopsy. I told her not to worry, it was okay; that I had assumed it was something serious.

This diagnosis is not what anyone wants to hear when they have taken every step to keep healthy. For years I had taken supplements and eaten a *supposedly anti-cancer diet* without many processed foods, and full of fruits and vegetables.

In my 73 years, apart from some minor illnesses and kidney stones (which had given me a good deal of trouble from time to time), I'd only had a broken wrist, and for a few years, I'd had a short bout of asthma; but thankfully that is long gone. I had no long-term physical problems I knew of; no regular aches and pains; and I was on no regular medication … I was *seemingly* fit and healthy!

I used to thank the Lord that I was so well and that I had no arthritis, no pain in my body and complete freedom of movement. Looking back, however, at that time there had been some tell-tale signs that I was unwell. For a few months I had been feeling a lack of enthusiasm for things I had previously enjoyed, and a much greater tiredness than normal. On a ministry trip to Doncaster to teach our course called 'Naturally Supernatural,' although we had a fruitful time with the Chinese Christian church there, I felt unusually tired.

Then back home, one day as I was loading shopping into the car at our local supermarket, I thought that I was going to collapse! I just felt so weak and tired. However, I thought… I simply needed a nap… or maybe I was just feeling my age!

In hindsight, when thinking about that string of urine infections… could they have been because I had a lowered immune system and nothing much to fight infection within me? Could it have been the same low immune system that had enabled the cancer to grow?

When I saw the oncology consultant, he was very pleasant, but he was also very honest. Although he pointed out the seriousness of my condition, he spoke very kindly and was seemingly positive about the outcome of treatment.

He said; *"You are very seriously ill. You have stage four Lymphoma, but I can kill it. I can cure it and give you your life back; and although your age is against you, I have been doing this for thirty years with great success. If you don't have the treatment, I could keep you going on steroids for a month, maybe two, but you will get weaker and weaker and die."*

It was chilling news to hear. I sat and tried my best to digest what this man was saying to me.

He offered me six treatments of something called *R-CHOP* to deal with this aggressive disease. Each session would be given 21 days apart. This is a combination of five substances that deal with the B cells which are the antibody factories of the body. One substance, the R, is delivered intravenously by a drip and the other four by the nurse very slowly using a syringe. What he didn't mention until later was the very scary intrathecal injection, an injection into my spine, which sends the chemo around my brain, so that nothing can escape and hide in that area and grow later.

I told him that I couldn't agree to have the treatment straight away and that I needed a week to consider it. I knew that must have sounded ridiculous to him, especially as he'd told me that without treatment I might have very little time left to live, but I knew that I couldn't undertake any treatment unless I had peace about it, and had faith that it was the right thing to do. However, there was something about the man, his honesty, coupled with kindness, that touched my heart that day and I thought; "*I think I can trust this man.*"

As I hesitated about the treatment, he looked away from me and said: "*I think you are a very brave woman and you are a lot sicker than you care to admit.*" However, I did know I was indeed *very* sick, and had been trying to convince several doctors for some weeks that I was sick, to no avail; although of course I did not realise that I might literally be on the brink of death.

To say that I was devastated by this diagnosis would be an understatement. When the consultant had left the room, I sobbed uncontrollably with the nurse who had also been present during the consultation. When I had calmed down, she said very kindly; "*Perhaps you could think of it like this – think how many people you will be able to help when you are out the other side of this.*"

Although she knew we were Christians and had been pastors of a church, she had no idea of our lifestyle of living with other people, of helping people in an in-depth way, and being intimately involved in so many people's lives. After telling her how we had lived our lives for almost 50 years, having over 60 people to live with us, she said; "*You certainly do know the score, don't you!*" She also told me how one of her children had been very sick and had overcome cancer. Then she said of the consultant.... "*I would trust this man with my life!*"

After the appointment, I was shaken and felt a little numb. A few days later, I received this letter from the consultant...

'*I reviewed Mrs Cornell as a new patient in the lymphoma clinic this afternoon...*' (after a few other complicated remarks about how it all presented when he examined me) he said; '*I can feel the lymphoma as an internal prominent mass.*'

'*Mrs Cornell has been a Christian pastor for 25 years and has a strong deep-held belief in the power of prayer. She is very reluctant indeed to consider chemotherapy for her lymphoma. I tried to discuss chemotherapy in a very open way. Of course, there are difficulties with chemotherapy, but we treat many patients every year with R-CHOP chemotherapy and we are able to cure many patients with her type of lymphoma.*

'*The disease is moving quite quickly and considering her recent symptoms and considering the extensive nature of her disease seen on the PET scan from two days ago, unfortunately I feel that without chemotherapy, her life expectancy would be limited to a few months and unfortunately as she presented initially with pain, then pain is likely to become a more dominant feature.*

'*With chemotherapy there is a very good chance of response and I would say that it is as high as 80% with resolution of her symptoms. Unfortunately, high grade lymphoma can relapse and overall, the long-term chance of curing high grade lymphoma in a 73-year-old woman with iPI4 degrees is best considered around 50%.*

'*I have put a prescription of Prednisolone, Allopurinol and Omeprazole on the hospital pharmacy and I have asked her to come back next week for these tablets that are there for her to take if she agrees to do so.*

'I was also very open with her. If she does not want to have chemotherapy then we of course cannot treat her but we will do our best to manage her symptoms over the coming months as she deteriorates.

'With best wishes.'
George

I felt that what the consultant had said was good as well as bad news, but some of those phrases struck fear into my heart. He had of course assumed that without treatment I would simply deteriorate, rather than get better. However, if I refused the treatment it would be because I believed that I was going to be well simply by prayer, and possibly with some alternative treatment, not because I thought I was going to deteriorate and die! To be really honest, at this point in time I was so weak and ill, that I thought momentarily that dying might be a good option!

I knew I had to shake that thought out of my mind as fast as it came in. I wouldn't want to abandon my husband, and I had also received prophecies from many sources which encouraged me not to give up just yet, because God had more for me to do in the future.

When considering whether to take this severe treatment, with all the potential risks, I knew that I had an enormous hurdle to jump. I have never thought of chemotherapy being the best option, preferring natural remedies, which I had researched for many years... and I had often said that I would never consider doing chemotherapy. However, as the consultant's letter said, I also believed passionately in the power of prayer and the healing power of God's Holy Spirit, so I knew God could do it!

CHAPTER 2

Yes, I do know God can do it!

I am no stranger to the healing power of God, I know that he can do wonderful things, and many times He has touched my body with His healing power. It was not hard for me to believe he could heal me at this time without any medical treatment. I have known many people with cancer and other diseases healed by the prayer of faith. I have also had a hand in bringing healing to others.

I remember one day back in 1974 when we lived in Sun Street, Isleham, God had clearly told me that His desire was to heal me, and He also commissioned me to bring physical and emotional healing to others.

As I was walking down the stairs that day, I heard God clearly say to me; *"Go into the sitting room; I want to speak to you. Find your bible and look up Isaiah 61."*

I immediately did what I was told, I opened my Bible to the passage and it read:

'*The Spirit of the Lord GOD is upon Me, Because the LORD has anointed Me to preach good tidings to the poor; He has sent Me to heal the broken-hearted, to proclaim liberty to the captives, and the opening of the prison to those who are bound; to proclaim the acceptable year of the LORD.*' Isaiah 61:1

After I'd read it, I clearly heard God say...

"This is what I want to do for you, and this is what I want you to do for others."

I was a little puzzled but I said; *"Thank you Lord. I don't know how you will do this or when you will do it... but thank you!"*

Back then, I was a new Christian with very little knowledge of the Bible, and I had no idea that this was the very Scripture Jesus quoted at the start of His ministry. Of course, I now know that this very Scripture was His own manifesto, and that later He called all his disciples to the same ministry. I think that in those days if I had realised that, I might have felt rather daunted!

Again, as a new Christian I had no idea that it was possible for God to heal me. One day as I was going to the doctor with a sore throat, just as I got into the car, I thought... *'I wonder if God would heal me if I asked Him...'* then I thought... *'no, I don't think that He would be bothered about my trivial sicknesses.'*

How wrong can you be when you don't know the word of God!

The complete opposite has been true in my life with God. Thankfully, I've learned a few things over the years about God's interest in the smallest details of our lives. Since that time, I have had many experiences of God being involved in healing sickness in my life.

Here are some of the amazing instances of His interventions which I'm recounting as I believe they will encourage you to trust God for your own healing.

Once I received my healing simply by listening to a tape recording of healing Scriptures. I had returned home after visiting people in Northampton, earlier than planned, because I had developed every symptom of flu. I drove home feeling terrible and fell into bed. I put on a cassette tape of Kenneth Hagin speaking healing Scriptures. When I'd listened a few times to each side, I suddenly **heard** these words. They went off in my heart with a bang!

'But for you who fear my name, the Sun of righteousness will rise with healing in his wings, and you will go free, leaping with joy like calves let out to pasture.' Malachi 4:2 NLT

At that **very** moment, I was completely healed! Every symptom left my body! It took me a few moments to take in what had happened, but as I lay there feeling completely well, I decided to get up, get dressed and go down to the kitchen. I had just started to load the dishwasher when someone came into the room and was very surprised to see me up and about, and said; *"I thought you were sick?"*

I gave them a broad smile; *"Well, I was,"* I said, *"but now I'm healed!"*

Another time I had a visitation from Jesus to my hospital bed after I'd had a kidney stone surgically removed. This time the story is much more involved and is a process… as healing often is.

This healing *'adventure'* began when I decided that I needed to ask the Lord to get rid of my kidney stones. It had been suggested to me that as they grew bigger an operation was likely. As I really didn't want an operation, I asked the vicar and a group of friends from our church to gather and to pray that God would move the stone. So, very simply this little group anointed me with oil and prayed that God would move the stone.

First mistake! I should have asked that God would dissolve the stone! But we were at that point, just taking baby steps in a walk of faith!

Within a week I was wracked with pain in my lower back on the side where I knew that the stone was. However, the doctor had told me that because this stone was in a blind ended tube in the kidney, due to a condition called *Medullary sponge kidney*, it could never come out naturally, it could only come out with an operation.

I was convinced that the stone had moved because I was in such agony, it felt like razor blades being drawn through my body, so I asked Tony to pray that the stone would stop moving. He did and it did! However, I soon realised that if it were true, that the stone had moved, the stone would now obviously be stuck halfway down the urethra which might not be a very healthy situation!

Evidently, it was stuck there because I soon began to have a high temperature and felt terribly ill, but because of the medical diagnosis of the stone being in a blind ended tube I could not persuade the doctor that the stone had moved and was given several lots of antibiotics until eventually I point blank refused to have any more and asked for a scan. I went into Addenbrookes for the scan on a Friday. It confirmed what I already knew: that the stone was definitely not in the kidney anymore but stuck in the urethra, it was halfway out! I caught sight of the kidney in the scan, it was much enlarged with the trapped waste liquid and it looked very alarming, as if it could burst at any moment!

It was obvious why it was making me feel so ill, because the toxins that should have been passed from my body were feeding back into my system, making me feel very weak and often on the point of collapse. Consequently, I was booked to go back to the hospital on the following Monday to have the stone surgically removed.

I was assured that the operation was a much simpler job, because the stone was not in the kidney, I wondered if we should pray again and ask God to take the stone out of my body the rest of the way or whether I should go in for the surgery. I asked God to speak to me clearly about what to do. I asked him to speak to me in the Sunday morning service. In the middle of all this, I went to church in Chippenham on the Sunday morning, very attentive because I expected God to speak to me in some way: and He did!

One of the readings was from Genesis and was about Joseph when he was in charge of everything in Egypt, having an encounter with his fearful brothers. Joseph had looked after them very well up until then, but when their father died, they feared that Joseph would turn on them and kill them. They were terrified. When they came grovelling before him expressing their fear, he said to them; "...*Do not be afraid, for am I in the place of God? But as for you, you meant evil against me; but God meant it for good, in order to bring it about as it is this day, to save many people alive. Now therefore, do not be afraid; I will provide for you and your little ones." 'And he comforted them and spoke kindly to them.'* Genesis 50:19-21

God spoke to me clearly through that Scripture, and I felt very excited! I just knew that God was telling me that going to the hospital was a good thing, and that He was sending me into the hospital to benefit someone else; so I went gladly!

When I arrived at the hospital, I was ushered into a waiting room full of people whom I thought must be waiting to be admitted to a ward. I wondered if '*my person*' was there. As I looked around the room a lady opposite me smiled. Then suddenly, I saw a light appear supernaturally over the top of her head, and I knew God was saying that she was the one! With so many people waiting, I wondered how I was going to get close enough to her to be of any help. I thought that I really needed to be in the bed next to her, so that we could get to know each other. I should have known better than to worry, as God always has these things in hand!

I was put in a ward with just three beds and, of course, there she was, right next to me. Her name also was Margaret and it transpired that she was terrified! A hole had been accidentally cut in her bladder when she had her womb removed recently and she had come in to have the damage repaired.

We had hardly been in the ward a few moments, when she turned to me and said: "*Why has God allowed this to happen to me?*" I have never had such a clear invitation to talk about God! Because of this medical mistake during her surgery, Margaret was understandably very frightened about being there. However, we got on like a house on fire, and I was able to pray with her and make her feel easier.

God, the one who thinks of every detail, had also made perfect provision for my husband and children in my absence. On the Friday on my way to the hospital, I had given Brian a lift into Cambridge: he was a young man that lived with us. I picked him up on the way back and told him that I was booked to go into the hospital on the Monday for an urgent operation. He then told me about the young woman he'd met that day called Laurette. She needed somewhere to stay in between trips with YWAM and what was more, she was a nurse!

We immediately fixed to meet her and instantly all fell in love with her. She was all set to look after the children and Tony whilst I was in hospital, and then to be there tending to me and the family when I came home from the operation needing to recuperate.

I went into surgery. After the operation I realised, when I'd felt ill before, it had been nothing! I felt absolutely terrible after the big operation, and the consensus of my visitors was that I was very ill indeed. I had a large painful scar, a drip and a drain, and nothing seemed to dim the pain. Every move I made was sheer agony! My new friend Margaret was now okay, and so now it was her turn to feel sorry for me, because I was in a great deal of pain and rather immobile.

On the third night I was waiting quietly for the nurse to come and turn the lights off in the ward, and suddenly I felt the presence of Jesus come into the room. I did not actually see His complete form or His likeness, but just like the disciples on some occasions when they met with Jesus in His resurrected form, I just knew that it was Him. I felt Him standing at the bottom of my bed. I felt Him touch my feet, and with a whoosh, I felt the power of God go right through my body and out of the top of my head, and as suddenly as He came, He was gone.

Immediately, I felt so warm and comfortable and completely free of pain, although, except for how I *felt*, I had no specific evidence at that moment that I was healed. In my heart, though, I knew without a doubt that I was healed, and soon fell peacefully asleep.

During the night I was suddenly awakened with terrible pain in my left side which was the opposite side to the operation. I heard this nasty voice say; "*Ah now you're in trouble. The other kidney has been under strain and is so damaged; it will collapse and will cause you more pain.*" I started to think; 'Oh no, that's terrible!' And just as I was beginning to feel sorry for myself, I suddenly realised who the voice belonged to.

I sat up in the bed as best as I could and said: "*Oh no you don't devil! I don't have to listen to your lies! In Jesus name leave me right now!*" And I promptly fell back to sleep.

When I awoke in the morning, I felt wonderful. I had such an amazing sense of wellbeing and comfort, so after a few moments I decided to test my healing. I got out of bed and stood up. I lifted my hands into the air and bent down and touched my toes. I even slapped the scar, but I had no pain whatsoever and complete ease of movement. So, it was very different from the previous day, when I could only crawl about, wincing with pain, which even morphine struggled to kill.

Margaret, my new friend in the next bed, was amazed and asked me what had happened. I told her and added that I'd be going home soon. She rejoiced with me. I said: *"We'll pray together before I go home."*

I had been sent a very large bouquet of flowers which were in a vase at the side of the ward. I picked them up with my arms stretched out and still without pain, I carried them out of the ward.

As I walked past the nurse's station to find some water to add to the vase, the nurses looked at me with total astonishment. I asked them; *"Where can I change the water in these flowers?"* A nurse simply pointed to a door across the corridor and said, *"Over there..."*

Soon the doctor came in to see me on his daily round with several students. He said: *"How are you today Mrs Cornell?"* I replied: *"I haven't felt so well for a long time!"* He looked very pleased; *"Didn't we do well!"* he said. *"Oh no,"* I said; *"It's not all your fault!"* I proceeded to tell him the story of Jesus' visitation.

He gave me a long hard stare, leaned over and looked at a sticker on my bible which said, *'Born Again'* and asked what it meant. I began to explain; but he said: *"I'm really sorry I haven't got time to hear any more but get your clothes on and go home."*

When the nurse came into the room, I told her what the doctor had told me to do. She said: *"Don't be silly he couldn't have said that."* She went off to check it out and came back and said: *"He did say that... come on we need to get that drip and that drain out right away!"*

As she did so, I recounted my story of Jesus' visit and when I went back to the ward, I felt an urgency to pray with my fellow inmate. I had no natural idea how or when I was going to get home, but in my heart, I just knew it was imminent. As we prayed and said *'amen'* another person behind me said *amen* too! When I turned to look, I was delighted to see that it was a lady who went to our church and lived in the next village. She had come in on the off chance that they would let her see me. I said to her; *"Could you please take me home now?"* And she did.

When I arrived home, our new nurse friend, Laurette was very surprised to see me, and in her beautiful Swiss French accent said; *"Margaret, you are not behaving like a sick person!"* *"Mmm..."* I smiled; *"Well that's because I'm not a sick person, I'm a healed person!"*

There was considerable surprise expressed when I saw other people who had seen me the day before, in hospital. I had great fun witnessing to anyone in the village I came across about what had happened.

I remember another time when I was troubled with a yet another kidney stone. I actually delivered myself of it painlessly, simply by praying in tongues. I was in the usual agony that a moving stone causes and was just about to say to Tony that I should go to the hospital, when I remembered what happened in the walled city in China. Jackie Pullinger in her book called *'Chasing the Dragon,'* reported how she got addicts delivered painlessly from heroin by making them pray in tongues until they were through the withdrawal symptoms of the drug. As I thought about that, I just began to pray in tongues. After a considerable while, the pain left. I fell asleep and, in the morning, I had passed the stone.

In my 40's when I had developed asthma, I had inhalers and saw the nurse at the surgery regularly for a couple of years. All the while though, I was praying to receive healing and expecting God to do it. Then I was recommended by a friend, that as well as praying, I should take some *'green'* supplements, which I think were things like spirulina. Over a period of time, I was healed of asthma, I believe by the combination of prayer and those *'green'* supplements. It seems that when we've done all **we** can, then God does all He can!

On another occasion, I was also supernaturally healed of a dislocated jaw, which, believe it or not, I had dislocated eating a flapjack! I know it sounds an unlikely event, but at our village coffee morning, after I had eaten one delicious flapjack, I was tempted to eat another. I felt a little nudge from the Holy Spirit warning me not to do so. but it was one of those *easily ignored* little nudges from Him, and it was soon too late. That wonderfully gooey biscuit soon had my teeth glued together, As I struggled to free my teeth that were glued together by this delicious biscuit, I hurried out of the room, and in freeing myself I wrenched the jaw out of its socket...For ages I prayed, and had others pray for me but to no avail.

It would slip into place and then out again. One day a friend looked at me compassionately as I told her about it; she reached out her hand, touched my cheek gently and said quietly; "*In Jesus name, be healed!*" And I was! It never slipped out again, and years later is perfectly okay.

I had also seen many people wonderfully healed by prayer.

I had preached and taught healing for forty years, and I was part of a team who ran Healing Rooms in Ely for ten years. Before I became sick, I had been preaching healing wherever I went. I even did so when we were on a holiday cruise in 2017. One day we began talking to a waitress, she discovered that we were ministers, and was overjoyed! She asked; "*Would you be prepared to minister to our crew at our late-night meeting?*" Of course, we were delighted to accept!

I was astounded to see that this event had been prophesied to me by Cindy Jacobs in the previous May at a ladies meeting in London and that I was now seeing the beginning if its fulfilment. Here is what she said...

'I am doing a work in you that you can only imagine. For there were former doors that were open that are now seemingly closed, but the Lord says; I am opening doors, doors that cannot be shut. I am giving you a

key of influence which will allow you to go behind closed doors into secret places and I'm going to give you the entree and what you need. This isn't your former place – it's your new place. (Then she shouted) *THIS IS YOUR NEW PLACE!'*

At these powerful words, I fell to the ground, being slain in the spirit. I was out for the count… touched by God and so blessed!

Now, here we were in the Mediterranean, on holiday, being taken into the crew's private quarters on the ship! They had to get special permission for us to do this and give us a special pass. Late that night, one of the crew came to fetch us and escorted us to the meeting. As we went through a door marked CREW ONLY, and into an inner door beyond, I said; *"This is my prophecy fulfilled. I'm now going behind closed doors into secret places!"*

A few years later, we went on another cruise around the Caribbean with the same cruise company and met up with the same waitress who engaged us for a meeting yet again! It was then that I had preached healing. We had a wonderfully powerful meeting followed by the laying on of hands with powerful results. The interesting thing was that this second time of ministry would not have fulfilled the prophecy as it was held in one of the public rooms! God is so accurate!

In 1 Timothy 1:18; we are told to **'wage the good warfare'** with the prophecies that God has given us, which we can do by meditating on them and keeping them alive in our hearts. They are purveyors of hope and builders of faith.

In this crisis situation I was now fully focused on His promises and every prophecy I'd had that I could remember, and ready to go into battle with them! All these extraordinary experiences of God's help and all the encouraging words I'd received, were saved in my *'faith bank,'* assuring me that I could ask God to heal me with confidence, and that He would do it!

CHAPTER 3

But...would God heal *my* cancer?

The question for me was not really *would God heal my cancer*, but **how** did He want to do it do it. I needed to make a very important decision: whether or not to take medical treatment. I urgently needed to know what God was saying to me at this very moment in time.

In our 25 years of ministry I had known people healed of cancer with medical treatment and prayer. I had known others who refused medical treatment and were healed supernaturally. I knew many who accepted treatment, seemed to believe in God's healing power and still died. We had walked through it with them all so I knew the difficulties and the agonies of the sickness and the treatment. It was not something I relished the thought of doing. I did not want to accept medical treatment because of unbelief or fear; neither did I want to refuse treatment blindly as a '*faith*' issue. We always need to know the mind of God in every situation. If we know His will, even if the situation is difficult, we can have peace in our heart as we face it.

My first step, as the bible instructs us, was to ask the elders of the church to agree with me for a miracle. As it says in James 5:13-15; '*Is anyone among you suffering? Let him pray. Is anyone cheerful? Let him sing psalms. Is anyone among you sick? Let him call for the elders of the church, and let them pray over him, anointing him with oil in the name of the Lord. And the prayer of faith WILL save the sick, and the Lord will raise him up. And if he has committed sins, he will be forgiven.*'

I really believed that was true and that I could truly expect a miracle! For me it was a moving moment, when all but one of the elders, who wasn't there that day, anointed me with oil, prayed and agreed with me for that miracle. I did not receive the outward manifestation of a miracle healing at that precise moment but in my heart, I received my healing, knowing that the Bible says that we must believe that we receive our answer *when we pray* not when we see the results!

I have to say here; that if I'd been the average Christian; at that moment I might have thought a number of things. I could have concluded that God no longer heals today. Or I could have thought, "it's obvious that God doesn't want to heal me". I could have walked away disillusioned and disappointed; but I didn't, because I knew that if I kept my faith steady that the moment of receiving would come. We all want that instant miracle, and it does happen; but often healing is a process, and we need to live expectant for that moment to come.

However, even if healing did not come, I was not afraid of dying. As I have said, when I had felt so very ill, I had briefly considered it as an attractive option. Going to be with Jesus sounded great rather than pushing through to the place of healing, but I rejected it immediately, because I felt that God had promised me a future and a hope. I had too many unfulfilled prophecies on my life!

I believe that we should do all we can do in the natural to help ourselves and that after we have done all we can do; God will do the rest!

So, after prayer, I immediately contacted a man I knew that seemed to understand both medical and natural cancer treatments and I booked a telephone consultation with him. It was supposed to be a twenty-minute call, but we were talking for at least an hour! He gave me details of supplements and all the possible kinds of treatments I could have. He was very helpful, and in the end, he said; "*Look, people think I'm against medical treatment, but actually I'm against people taking it in ignorance. If you decide to take the treatment, keep to your diet and take the supplements anyway, which will increase your chance of success. Come back to me afterwards and I will help you rebuild your immune system."*

Of course, whatever I decided I was going to pray and trust God; but I knew that I had three options. I could accept the treatment offered by the NHS and pray; I could possibly go to a clinic in Mexico or the U.S.A or Germany, for natural treatment and pray; or I could pray and *'wing it'* on supplements and a strict healthy diet. At that moment I just did not know which of those ways was the right way to go.

I had been much encouraged the previous year by supporting a young woman in our church who was diagnosed with an inoperable brain tumour. She was very ill, but after seeking God very carefully, she refused medical treatment of any kind. I was able to support her in this because the Holy Spirit confirmed to me and her husband that this was the right thing for her to do. She also consulted our nutritionist friend, changed her diet, exercised, confessed the Word, prayed fervently and has been wonderfully healed! She looks better now than she had looked for many years. I and many others had some amazing times ministering to her. She was one of the small number of people whom I have supported who did everything that I and others suggested to beat cancer, trusting God and without medical treatment.

I never had a moment's doubt that, by whatever means I chose, if it was God's choice then I would be healed. I knew that I was in God's hand and that all **was** well ... and I was fully prepared to go ahead without medical help.

You may wonder, how could I be so sure of being healed? First of all, I was sure of my healing, because the Word of God says it is His will for me to be healed, and God is always faithful to His Word. To back it up, I had all those wonderful experiences of God's previous work in my life and all the wonderful things I've seen Him do for others in my faith bank .But I knew that I was unable to make the right decision by myself simply on my natural circumstances, and the offer of medical help or on the advice and experience of others. I had to know what God thought at that particular moment in time. You need that assurance too.

There have been very few times since I became a Christian when I have not taken time to listen to what God wanted to say about an important issue. When I have failed to listen to what He has to say, things have not turned out well at all. But I knew that I could trust Him to speak to me clearly about what I should do in this instance. So, I spent that precious week before my next hospital appointment seeking God for His will in the matter.

I knew that there were many ways in which God could speak to me.

He could use the still small voice within my heart.

He could give me dreams and visions.

He could speak through others who hear Him and know Him.

He could speak to me through His word as I read it.

Maybe he would speak to me in an audible voice, as He has done occasionally.

Sometimes He has simply given me a deep inner peace about things. I was open to them all; and then I would look for confirmation from others, whom I knew heard God, especially my husband.

For more than thirty years I have learned to listen to God's voice and then write down what I believe He is saying, or as we call it, "journal".

First, I ask God a question, get my heart quiet and then write. So, during this week, I spent time seeking Him. It is my custom when I sit down to journal to ask God to give me a picture of where He is. I would say: "*Show me where you are, Jesus, and what you are doing*". This day, as I focused my attention on Him, looking and listening I wrote these words from my heart...

'Lord, I find myself in the valley of decision – but not torn between two decisions as I thought I might be. I just feel suspended. But I'm not afraid or anxious in any way. I know that I am safe in the palm of your hand and that your hand is upon me. In your presence I feel such security and almost feel that whatever I decide to do… you will take care of it. I am overwhelmed by people's response to my news and never believed that this would happen to me. I am looking for a strong inner witness about my choices, as I know I cannot be persuaded by natural circumstances. Of course, I would like you to heal me without the treatment, as I know that you are greater than lymphoma and it must bow the knee to you.

Ringing in my heart right now I have the words of that song, 'I am no longer a slave to fear...I am a child of God,' and I can only picture you, Jesus, fast asleep in Peter's boat, totally unfazed by the storm.'

The picture I saw of Jesus fast asleep in the back of Peter's boat with the storm raging all around was so powerful! He was at peace in that storm on the lake of Galilee, unlike the disciples whom it seemed were in a complete panic. The terrified disciples woke Jesus up saying; *'Teacher, do you not care that we perish?'* Mark 4:38. When I saw that Jesus *'wasn't bothered,'* I knew that it wasn't that He didn't care about me. I saw clearly that He was saying that although my situation might seem like a storm, that He wasn't unduly bothered by it, because just as He was master of that storm on Galilee, He was master of my storm too! At that moment, I let go of all the care of it, and never worried about the cancer again. I knew that He would deal with it!

However, because cancer seems like such a giant, I felt that it was somewhat different from other sicknesses, which hadn't the ability to end my life. It's easy to accept the non-life-threatening types of sickness, be quite casual about them and tolerate them. It's not a good idea to do that... but we do!

As I prayed about what to do and was thinking what a giant cancer seems to be, I thought of the Bible account that tells of how David was able to face Goliath... *his* giant. He could face Goliath with faith because he'd already '*killed the lion and the bear.*' I realised that the previous healing that I had experienced were like *my* lion and *my* bear. Like David, I knew I had a covenant with God. His was an Old Testament one, but I knew that mine is made with the shed blood of Jesus. The book of Hebrews assures me that the covenant I have is a better covenant. David knew Goliath was weak because he did not have a covenant with God, thus he called him, '*this uncircumcised Philistine.*' 1 Samuel 17:26 So, I knew that I could rely fully on that wonderful covenant that I am party to!

I knew that I needed to cooperate with God, but I knew that the effectiveness of my covenant, although activated by my faith, does not actually rely on my sinlessness and perfection. I can relax in Him because the fulfilment of my covenant relies on Christ's sinlessness and perfection. What a relief that is!

David's revelation of his covenant and his previous experiences made him bold and fearless and this same knowledge made me fearless too. Why should I not have the same confidence as David had in his God... in my GOD? If I chose to take the treatment, I knew that I would not be trusting in the treatment to heal me. I knew that it would be God Himself who would do it, and I was determined that God would get the glory for it. It was HIS battle not mine. As it says in Zechariah 4:6; '*Not by might not by power, but by My Spirit, says the Lord!*'

Therefore, I decided that I would never say that I was fighting cancer, I knew that as I put my faith in that precious covenant, His anointing and His Word were fighting it. David similarly knew that the battle was the Lord's, as he says; *'Then all this assembly shall know that the LORD does not save with sword and spear; for the battle is the LORD's, and He will give you into our hands.'* 1 Samuel 17:47 Like David, I was utterly sure that God by His Spirit would have the victory.

Jesus told us that a combination of prayer, faith and action, builds a foundation in our lives that cannot be destroyed by circumstances. As it says in Luke 6:47-49; *'Whoever comes to Me, and hears My sayings and does them, I will show you whom he is like: He is like a man building a house, who dug deep and laid the foundation on the rock. And when the flood arose, the stream beat vehemently against that house, and could not shake it, for it was founded on the rock. But he who heard and did nothing is like a man who built a house on the earth without a foundation, against which the stream beat vehemently; and immediately it fell. And the ruin of that house was great.'*

So, remembering my covenant with God was really important to me because many times I'd taught about the covenants of the Bible, and I knew that God says that once he has sworn a covenant, He will **never** go back on it.

Part of my covenant is expressed in Isaiah 54:17. *'"No weapon that is formed against you shall prosper, and every tongue which rises against thee in judgment you will condemn. This is the heritage of the servants of the LORD, and their righteousness is of Me," says the LORD.'*

As we live in a fallen world and satan is the god of this world's system, so there will always be weapons that are formed against us; but this is a clear promise, that they will **not** prosper. In other words, they will not succeed. Jesus Himself warned us that; *'in the world you will have tribulation.'* John 16:33

As I waited for God to speak to me on another occasion, He said to me...

'I am Love my child, and there is no fear in love. This is why you have peace, because my love is within you as well as surrounding you, holding you steady from the outside. Always be conscious of who I am in you – you are my temple, my dwelling place, where you have made a home for me. Be assured that I will not see my home destroyed by a disease that I took upon myself on the cross... that I personally bought at such a great price. I paid dearly for it. It is my privilege and my joy to cleanse the temple and restore you to perfect health.'

When I had told the consultant I was trusting God, he had said; *"Perhaps God will use me to do it."* I knew God could use the treatment; but I needed to be sure that it was the right thing to take the chemotherapy.

During that week of searching, when I asked the Lord if I should take the treatment I'd been offered, I felt God planted in my heart two clear Scriptures. The first one was the words of Jesus in Mark 16:18; *'If they drink anything deadly, it will by no means hurt them.'* Then God led me to the passage in Acts 28 where Paul was bitten by a poisonous snake and shook it off, having no ill effects. It was obvious that the power of God in him was greater than the poison in the snake bite. I felt God say that the anointing in me would be stronger than the poisonous chemotherapy. So, as the treatment would mean allowing terrible poisons into my system, these seemed very pertinent Scriptures.

Then two friends, whose spiritual judgement I trust, gave me the same Scripture, saying that if I took the treatment I would suffer no permanent harm.

Then, to crown it all, one morning that week as I got up, I clearly heard God say in an audible voice: *"When you go through the fire you will not be burned."* (Isaiah 43:2) That was enough for me... my heart was settled. I felt safe.

After this, as if I needed more confirmation, Joseph, a church leader at Lighthouse sent me this confirming word about the treatment; *"God will use medicines and whatever he has put into human hands to perfect your healing. Remember man was created to conquer and dominate the earth. I believe God will use men and medicines to bring His will of healing to you... in Jesus name."*

'Many are the afflictions of the righteous, but the LORD delivers him out of them all.' Psalm 34:19

He continued; *"Keep seeing the cancerous cells removed as the chemotherapeutic medicines go into your body."*

I certainly will! I now had solid faith to take the treatment, and I knew that whatever I had the faith to do would work. I just had to be sure that I had taken the right option! My friend Rebecca echoed this thought: *"Your trust in Him counts beyond the means itself."*

During this same week, my husband Tony was obviously exercising great self-control and wisdom, as he said nothing to influence me. He wanted me to have the freedom of hearing God for myself, but he was greatly relieved when I told him that I had decided to take the treatment and he agreed that I should do so. Although he is a man of faith, later he said that during that week he had to combat the fear of losing me to cancer.

When I went back to the hospital to report what I'd decided to do about the treatment, I saw a different consultant who seemed uncomfortable and almost ready to be aggressive with me. I suppose he was expecting me to be difficult and say that I was not going to have the treatment. I can only imagine what he would have said if I'd refused the treatment! A friend of mine who had refused treatment for bladder cancer received the most horrible and upsetting letter from the consultant assuring her that she would certainly die. She didn't!

We sat down and to my surprise he suddenly banged the table and said loudly; "*You WILL lose all your hair!*" Startled, I said: "*Oh, well I'm not as concerned about that as I was about what it might do to my internal organs. Losing my hair seems trivial in comparison.*" Before he could say any more, I said; "*Look I've decided to take the treatment!*" At which point he calmed down, and wordlessly he pushed the consent form towards me, which I signed in quite an awkward silence.

After that interview when I was all signed up, knowing I could possibly lose my hair, we went to Maggie's, a charity which has premises on the hospital site. Maggie's provides counselling, exercise courses, hospitality, and hats and wigs free of charge for cancer patients. It's a lovely homely place where they quickly offer you a drink and refreshments and are ready to give you kindness and support. I was very glad to go there at that moment when I had signed myself up for the chemotherapy and also it was a haven of peace when I had time gaps in my treatment schedule. It felt very welcome. That day, because I still had my hair, I was able to choose a lovely wig which was the same colour and the same style as my own hair. It's so convincing that when I wore it, often people would say; "*You didn't lose your hair, then!*"

I knew that the treatment was not an easy option, but I knew that almost nothing could steal the peace I had in my heart because '*Faithful and absolutely trustworthy is He who is calling you [to Himself for your salvation], and He will do it. [He will fulfil His call by making you holy, guarding you, watching over you, and protecting you as His own].*' 1 Thessalonians 5.23 Amplified Bible.

CHAPTER 4

Now I know what to do...

The date was fixed for a week's time for the treatment to begin.

My sons were obviously very concerned at what I had told them, and both showed me as much support as they were able to do. Before I started the treatment, my son Ben showed how much he cared by driving all the from Glastonbury with his two children, Blaize, who was three, and Leonora, aged eight. I felt so ill and didn't really feel up to having visitors but nonetheless I welcomed them. They are lovely children and Ben is a good dad, so it was a wonderful comfort to see them. My other son, Giles who lives nearer prayed for me and came to see me often and sometimes took me to the hospital for appointments and treatments.

I didn't want them to be worried, but I was so glad that they cared about me. I began the treatment with confidence, but I soon discovered that it was certainly not a straightforward journey that I was on.

What a roller coaster ride it turned out to be!

After the first treatment day, which seemed to go smoothly, after a few days I realised that all was not well. I began to feel very ill indeed. I had a high temperature and flu-like symptoms. I was alternately shivering and sweating, so I rang the chemo nurse as I'd been instructed to do if such a thing occurred. She insisted that I go to the hospital immediately. At the hospital, I spent four miserable days being barrier-nursed. They gave me huge doses of intravenous antibiotics and so many blood tests; I thought they considered me a pin cushion! It was a bleak time, with very few visitors. I felt lonely and quite desolate.

They sent me home with two lots of strong antibiotics. On the first night home, I woke up in the night having very violent and very copious diarrhoea. It was *everywhere...* on the bed, all down my legs, all over the floor, right into the bathroom. It was distressing, having to change the bed, wash out my pyjamas, have a shower and clear it all up. But most distressing of all for me was to see Tony at two o'clock in the morning, scrubbing the cream carpet in the hall on his hands and knees so that it would not be permanently stained. When I told the doctor about the problem the next day, he told me to stop taking one of those tablets, and from then on, I was fine!

Christmas didn't seem to hold much promise of good things. It felt a bleak prospect. There were no comforting family invitations and I didn't feel much like eating anything or cooking anything... but despite it all God surprised us with a lovely Christmas Day.

In the morning we went to our pastor Paul's home for breakfast. Later, Gill, my next-door neighbour, despite having a house full of guests herself, very kindly brought us two plates of a super Christmas meal.

There was no respite though, because on Boxing Day, when I woke up I discovered that I had developed a huge lump behind my knee which was so painful that I couldn't bear weight on my leg and could only walk with a stick. We were invited to visit friends that day, and I could barely hobble from the car into the house. When I was seated, it didn't feel too bad. We prayed a lot and spent time in worship; and we managed to have a great day.

Two days later Tony dropped me off outside the hospital; I was in agony with the lump. I staggered into the foyer of the hospital, where a very kind volunteer found a wheelchair and pushed me down the long corridor to the oncology department. When I went into my appointment with the consultant, he exclaimed with amazement; *"You're in a wheelchair?"*

He thought that the lump could be a Baker's cyst or a blood clot. I was promptly sent for a scan, and it did indeed turn out to be a blood clot or a thrombosis, which resulted in my having blood thinning injections into my belly until the chemo treatment was over. God bless a nurse friend Sarah, and Tony, who administered most of them for me, as I was too cowardly to do it myself!

The second treatment went without any further difficulty, and there was no further infection or any other unusual problem afterwards. At this stage though, I was also still having some intermittent pain which disturbed us for a couple of nights, but now, thankfully, I had morphine to hand!

After the third treatment I could hardly believe it. I woke up one morning completely deaf! Again, I rang the emergency number and asked if this could be a side effect of the treatment. I thought it could be, as I was being given methotrexate injections into my spine, intrathecally, so that my brain got a dose of chemo too! The aim of this form of treatment was to catch any stray cells that might find a hiding place there.

I thought that this was a probably a great idea, but the first time I had this injection I must admit that I momentarily felt so terrified, that I shook all over and hot tears flew from my eyes. I thought, '*this has the potential to paralyse me if it is administered incorrectly!*' However, a kind nurse was there to hold my hand. She was very reassuring and explained how many checks and precautions were taken to make sure that it was safe. In all the six times I had that treatment ... all was well.

When I had felt gripped by that paralysing fear as they were preparing that spinal injection, I thought… *now is the moment I must really trust God. But also, at this moment I must trust Man!*

When I had rung Addenbrookes about the deafness, the nurse passed my inquiry on to a consultant who rang me back and said he'd never heard of any such side effect such as this and suggested I visited my GP. With a kind smile, my GP said adroitly; "*Well; it could be brain damage, but I don't think so!*" He drew me a little diagram of the inner ear and diagnosed it as a clogged Eustachian tube. He was right because after a few days it soon cleared. I was mightily relieved. ·

After the fourth treatment I had a horrible fall.

It was a Sunday morning. We were due to minister at the Anglican church in Stuntney. I was not able to go because of the risk of infection. At nine o'clock I was horrified to notice that Tony was not yet dressed to go to Stuntney for the service that starts at 9.30. So, I rather foolishly rushed anxiously from the bedroom, tripped over and fell flat on my stomach winding myself badly. I know how to fall from my stage days, and I know that you never put your hands out to stop yourself because your arms and wrists are liable to break if you do. I only did that once when we were on holiday in Cromer because I didn't want to get a new coat dirty and I have learned my lesson and will never do that again.

But the whole of the front of my body was very badly hurt. Whilst I was lying on the floor breathless and moaning in pain, Tony wanted to stay with me instead of going to Stuntney, but I wouldn't let him. Gary, our friend who stays with us sometimes, is a live-in carer and first-aid trained; and I knew he could help me. He took good care of me and wouldn't let me move until I felt okay and he'd checked me out. Then he showed me how to get up as he'd been taught to do, pulling myself up with the aid of a chair. He prayed for me, brought me a cup of tea and stayed with me until he knew I was fine. My body took a terrible blow that day and was very sore for some while; but I was not permanently damaged.

After all those unexpected and potentially very frightening twists and turns accompanying the treatment, I just got such a strong sense that satan was doing his very best to frighten me, but I was determined not to let him win! It was certainly proving to be a dirty fight!

Recently I was asking the Lord about his angels and the part they play in our lives, he confirmed to me that they were indeed busy in our lives, and he said...

"Remember how you loved that song 'His eye is on the sparrow and I know he watches me?' Well, I have watchers everywhere looking out for you. Remember that the song continues 'And I know that there are angels all around' You sang that, but now it is time to live it and realise that indeed my angels – my messengers - your guardians - are all around you, enfolding you in my love and my favour. I sent special healing angels with you to the hospital and that's the reason that you had a supernatural response to the treatment. They were there to bring a rapid recovery from the lymphoma. Be thankful that I and my heavenly hosts are with you."

I said to Him; "But Lord, what about all those horrible complications - the infection - the thrombosis - the deafness- the horrible fall? Were your angels not on duty then? And He replied to me…

"The enemy contended fiercely for your life because he knew that victory would release you to teach about me with fresh anointing and greater power. He was greatly afraid, but I the greater one, was contending with stronger arms, and defeat was sure for him."

Those days having the chemotherapy, apart from the injection in my spine, was not a problem for me. They had told me that the main side effect of the actual treatment was boredom.... which was true. It consisted of just spending all day connected to a drip. The first day this was very slow as they kept stopping it when I felt even slightly hot or unwell. After that, the nurse used four syringes to inject me with the chemotherapy drugs which took a further hour. Some days after that I had the injection in the spine, and other days I had to return the next day for it.

Those boring hours on those treatment days were always lightened by the refreshments orderly, who appeared just in time with a pleasant choice of sandwiches, fruit, yogurts and a drink. I wonder if these people realise what an important part they play in our lives at our time of trouble.

Dear friends also accompanied me, especially my friend Claire, who stayed for hours to '*hold my hand*' and was willing to run off and get me anything I needed. To fill the long hours, I read, I ate, I listened to sermons, I slept. I watched other people fascinated; wondering what was going on with them. Consequently, I avoided much of the boredom. The day always went very quickly and without undue problems. That is, except for the last treatment; when it took them virtually an hour to find an acceptable vein. They explained that hospital policy had changed, they had to look for veins on top of the arm where no veins are visible and not on the underside, where veins are obvious in most people. After a while of them poking about fruitlessly I was feeling quite queasy and had to ask them to give me break whist I recovered. I was so relieved that this had not happened on the first treatment. It was quite unnerving. The nurse was also shaking when she made the last attempt... I could see that she'd had enough too.

Every time I went; I was shocked at the number of people coming in for treatment. I felt very sorry for other patients, and often prayed for them. One day there was a particular old lady who was obviously in turmoil. I could see different staff spending time talking with her earnestly. Evidently it was about whether she should have a blood transfusion and risk offending her children. What agony! Perhaps they were Jehovah's Witnesses.

In this great sea of need, knowing that I am God's agent in every situation, I constantly looked for opportunities to witness about Jesus and pray for people. If there was an opening, I'd go for it. During my wait for one session, I overheard a man saying he was nervous about the injection into his spine. As I had only just had my first one the previous week, I spoke up and reassured him about it, and prayed for him.

One day I was waiting for my lift to come after my treatment and I sat with a man who was sitting in the waiting room looking quite depressed. He said; "*They've just told me there's no more they can do for me.*" I asked him whether, if he died, he knew where he would go. I told him that I was sure of my destination which was heaven and that it was because I knew Jesus as my Lord and Saviour. This was an ideal moment to share the gospel with him and encourage him to invite Jesus into his life, which I did gladly, although he didn't seem very interested. I think he was stunned by the news he had received but I hoped he would think later on, in the quiet of his home, about what I'd said.

On another occasion, when my friend Kirti and I arrived for the intrathecal injection, we saw a woman looking miserable and afraid, waiting outside the room for her turn. Immediately Kirti asked her if we could pray for her, which we did; and she was very grateful. Straight away her complexion changed from pale and wan to a beautiful rosy glow!

The treatment experience itself may have been okay, but the after-effects of it were horrible. I had a few days of energy created by steroids but after that, the tiredness set in with a vengeance. During those periods, I had to remind myself that before I had the treatment, I had been very ill, and I had also felt utterly terrible. There was obviously a fight going on in my body.

Although I didn't have all the possible side effects I could have had, like extreme nausea, I just felt utterly weak and exhausted, to the point that some days I could hardly stand or walk as my legs were so physically weak. We also had to get a commode because night-time trips to the toilet seemed unsafe on my wobbly legs. My head felt foggy; reading for any length of time was impossible. Even praying was hard. Many days I could get up only for a brief time in the mornings and go back to bed in the afternoon and sleep. There was also a constant battle with constipation: getting the dose of the Senna and the other medications right was a difficult juggling act.

As I wanted to spend good time in the Word of God, such extreme weakness and foggy brain was a concern because it robbed me of the ability to read. But I soon discovered I could say; "*Alexa: open the Bible and play a chapter of the Bible.*" And, bless her, she did! Or I listened to the Bible on my iPad. I also listened to many encouraging YouTube sermons and faith-filled podcasts. Each morning I usually got up, and I often watched Christian and sometimes secular television programmes which always cheered me up, and at other times I listened to a lot of healing scriptures and worship songs.

What consolation worship was! How it lifted my soul and my spirit! God ministered through worship to me like nothing else could. In just a few moments I was lifted out of pain and despair into the sweetness of God's presence. My friend Ali Loaker, in his book, '*Worship in the Storm*' says...

'*When we lift up the name of Jesus. he is enthroned upon our praises and the devil is dethroned and defeated. When we worship him even in the middle of adversity, great power is released and our worship becomes like a sword in our hand.'*

And how true it is when we sing, *'Turn your eyes upon Jesus, look full in His wonderful face, and the things of earth will grow strangely dim, In the light of His glory and grace.'*

When our focus is on Jesus, and He grows larger in our vision; we are lifted above our circumstances.

I tried to keep the focus off myself and on the Lord; and to pray for others with the same condition. I had been greatly inspired in 1982 by seeing Dodie Osteen in Texas speaking about her healing journey, from metastatic cancer of the liver. One of the things that she did, whether she felt like it or not, was to visit others and pray for them! Forty years later she is very beautiful and full of life.

CHAPTER 5

Food, exercise and small comforts

I already had no appetite and the treatment seemed to take away the rest of my appetite for most foods. Sadly, it was the healthy ones like salad that I couldn't face, which had been the elixir of life to me in the past. I had some juices and I loved home-made soup; I had a passion for a season for watercress soup. But I had to force myself to eat a proper meal. I knew that I had to eat something or anything I could, because I was not supposed to lose any more weight. Tony oversaw the kitchen and was always hopeful. He would say; "*What do you fancy today?*" Although I tried hard to like something, I would usually sigh and say, 'nothing.'

I had started off doing the healthy diet, the diet that I had studied for years, but I ended up eating almost everything that I wouldn't recommend. After a week or so struggling to do the healthy thing, I just couldn't face any of it. It summed it up when one day I cried out; "*I never want to see another chickpea in my life!*" I suppose, to me, the chickpea was the very symbol of the healthy diet.

The difficulty was that I seemed to have much less saliva and so I was only able eat things that were very liquid. The whole issue of diet had seemed a minefield. One day when I was in Addenbrookes, the dietician came and said that, because I had gallstones, I should eat low fat foods. The next day after the possible diagnosis of cancer, with attendant weight loss, I was told to eat lots of full fat foods!

Absolutely nothing tasted good, but I gladly ate small quantities of tinned fruit in fruit juice, yogurt, ice cream, and custard because it all just slipped down without effort. Sometimes I could manage a little scrambled egg. Most days I had mid-morning snacks of fresh fruit that Tony cut up for me, a small piece of toast or a croissant and very occasionally an afternoon treat of a tiny scone with jam and cream. I did enjoy lots of water, green tea and fruit juices.

Most days I would have eaten so little during the day, that in the night when I actually felt hungry I would get up and have a huge bowl of Crunchy Nut Cornflakes with lashings of creamy milk, something that horrified me. I would never have eaten this cereal at other times because it's so high in sugar, sugar being something which many say actually causes cancer.

The hospital gave me Fortisip drinks which each had 240 calories. I found them disgustingly sweet; but drank them very reluctantly, because when I didn't drink them, one week my weight plummeted again. I was appalled at much of what I was eating because I'd always thought that a healthy diet was really important.

I knew exercise was important, so, I prayed for an exercise bike. Soon after I had prayed, I was given one by a young couple we knew who saw my request on Facebook. However, my legs were so weak that I struggled to do even five minutes at a time. I did use our *wobble machine* a lot more, which required less effort, and I pinned the healing Scriptures up in front of it, so that I could confess them and meditate on them whilst exercising.

Chemotherapy certainly made me lose my hair bit by bit, and, to my surprise, from all over my body, but I had my lovely wig. My friend Stella brought me some beautiful turbans, which made me look a bit like the television cook Nadiya Hussain. I had a blue one, a purple one and a pink one. They were made of thick stretchy velvet material.

I considered these very elegant and they made me feel good. Tony thought that I looked like the girl in the famous painting, '*The Girl with the Pearl Earring*' when I was wearing my blue one. The likeness was quite good, I must admit; she's just much younger than I am!

I usually only wore the wig when I went out because it made me very hot and was a bit uncomfortable to wear for long periods of time. Later, I had a little rainbow hat, which was much thinner and less hot, as the weather became warmer. By June 2018, my hair was growing fast, and although it was rather thin, I knew I'd have to pluck up the courage to let it be seen by all. It was at that point in time delightfully fluffy and rather cute: like baby hair.

The treatment gave me some tingling and numbness in my feet. It was referred to as Peripheral Neuropathy, which apparently is due to nerve damage. However, when I mentioned it to the doctors, although they adjusted one of the chemo doses to stop it, they said that they were not concerned about it because it did not affect my mobility. It lasted months but now, at last, even that symptom has nearly gone. Medically speaking, they say it might never leave.

The initial sickness and the treatment put me out of action for around five months. It really did feel as if I had been taken hostage by it Sometimes, when I felt a bit better, I desperately wanted to go out. However, I had to be careful: even though I had injections into my belly for seven days after the treatment to cause my bone marrow to produce more white cells, due to the treatment my immune system was down, making me vulnerable to catching infections . Sometimes I was just too weak to do anything anyway. My muscles seemed to have very little strength in them, and on the rare occasions when I went out, I needed to use a stick for support. I could barely walk and standing for any length of time was difficult.

For some years Tony has had some weakness in his legs and I've been tempted to be a bit unsympathetic about it ... but now I understand perfectly, and feel great compassion for him.

One day I did manage to struggle to a shop in Newmarket and buy a lovely fluffy pink dressing gown. I thought that I'd better get it as quickly as possible, because I'd have much less use for it when I was well; so I made a supreme effort to go! I wore that cuddly dressing gown rather a lot and it was such a great comfort to me. Little things like that seemed to matter, in a way that at other times would have seemed insignificant.

I had much comfort from visits from friends and family, who sometimes had to cancel because they felt unwell. I was also sent some beautiful gifts which really blessed me; but most of the time it felt like a marathon journey in a very long, dark tunnel. I remember after treatment three, exclaiming; "I just can't do this anymore!" But I knew I had to keep going because I had committed to do it three times more!

Although I did not experience extreme mood swings, my feelings fluctuated. I mainly had joy and peace; but sometimes sad things would easily come to my mind from the past, and I would find myself crying about them. This sometimes made it feel a bit like a roller coaster ride!

I sometimes comforted myself during those dark moments that actually I *could* have been dead, but at least I could be glad that I was alive and could look forward to the end of the treatment. And when I thought how horrible the treatment was making me feel, it almost cheered me up to remember how very sick I had been, and how bad I'd felt even before I'd had the treatment. I realised that unless I'd had an out-and-out miracle, maybe without the treatment I'd still be in a battle.

I remembered a story that our friend Robert Maasbach told us about his mother, who encouraged herself by singing a hymn that was written by a man who lost his whole family in a shipwreck. When Robert was young, his father was often away ministering, leaving his mother to look after their six children. One day she scalded herself badly and was in a lot of pain. But from the upstairs he was moved to hear her singing '*It is well it is well; it is well with my soul.*' So, when things felt too hard, I too could encourage myself by singing the chorus of the hymn; whether I felt like it or not!

On the plus side I had supernatural results with the chemo, which clearly demonstrated the power of faith and prayer. After the first session I had a staggering 50% reduction of the Lymphoma and after the second treatment there was a further dramatic reduction. The doctors were impressed, and it was evidence to me, and I hope to them, that the hand of God was at work; a fact that I was eager to point out to them. However, one doctor said, "*Yes, of course, a positive mental attitude is very important.*"

Over the months I was so blessed to have had many strong, faith-filled anointed Christians pray with me, many who travelled a long way to see me. Each time I was prayed for, I expected that I would be completely delivered. Each time I was encouraged; and I certainly experienced some alleviation of the symptoms, and a new hope. It was, in my mind, only a matter of time before complete deliverance came. Therefore, I didn't let any visitors escape without praying for me!

The small victories I experienced were very sweet, and all the horrible effects of the treatment, and all the extra difficulties that occurred, could not rob me of the delight that I felt in the way God was so evidently helping me. It was always tough, but God kept reminding me that I wasn't doing it on my own. I could do it with Him, He spoke to me…

'You are my child – look how many times you have been crushed, and sat on, but you've never given up. My Holy Spirit is committed to making you ever faithful, ever strong and never able to give up. The language and the concept of defeat doesn't belong to you. In fact, your task is to make satan give up, to run and hide and be ashamed to show his face ever again. It is always a spiritual battle. Remember, when Philip died, how you committed to wipe satan off the face of the earth wherever you saw him. Always remember that you are not battling flesh and blood, and accompanied by My Spirit, my Word and My angels you are more than a match for our enemy the devil. He cannot win, he can only have a temporary victory because you know how to defeat him. Keep faithful and strong because you are on My winning side. You are my battleaxe and weapon of war. I have made you strong and powerful in my Spirit.'

So, there it is… whether I feel like it or not… victory is mine!

As God led me through His plan of action, I began to wonder…

How on earth did all this happen?

The Word says; *'If any of you lacks wisdom; let him ask of God, who gives to all liberally and without reproach, and it will be given to him'.* James 1:5

God doesn't mind us asking Him for wisdom, He is always ready to explain things to us when we don't understand. Yes, I was asking why God? But I certainly wasn't shaking my fists angrily at him saying, *'Why me, God?'*

I asked the Lord, *'Lord, how did I get sick? Show me how I allowed this into my body?'* I thought this was a very important question, because If I knew how it had got in, I would know how to keep it out after it had gone! After all, I believed that I had done everything I could do to keep cancer at bay. I had eaten as well as I could, and tried to walk closely with God, but He showed me that I had failed in two areas; exercise and properly processing painful emotions when I was going through a very difficult time: a time of great stress when everything seemed to be unstable in my world. Some research seems to show that stress is one of the major factors in allowing disease into our bodies and minds. The Bible agrees:

'Beloved, I pray that you may prosper in all things and be in health, just as your soul prospers.' 3 John:2

If all is not well in our soul, which we consider to be our mind, will and emotions, can all be well in our bodies?

God began to speak to me about getting rid of any hurt or pain in my heart, dealing with it, and then actively cultivating joy daily. When we do this we are not looking for someone or something to blame. We are just trying to discern what might be important for us to deal with. Maybe someone *has* done things that have hurt us but it's *our reaction* to what they have done that needs dealing with.

Gradually it was as if a light turned on, highlighting some of the significant incidents from the past. He showed me some decisions that Tony and I made that I felt were right to make by the Holy Spirit, but actually those decisions were very painful to me. My spirit was happy with them, but my soul was not happy with them. Despite those decisions having resulted in so many good and positive things, which I would not go back and change, I knew that the pain I felt about them at that time had to go!

When I had marshalled my thoughts about them succinctly, as an initial step towards healing my heart, I talked to Tony about them. I felt he understood deeply, and he hugged me and held me tight as I wept and wept until I could weep no more. Slowly I felt that the pressure of all the pain, and the terrible grief that those decisions had caused me to feel, went from my heart.

When I began to look back over the many painful experiences that I had gone through a couple of years previously, I was not surprised that I had become sick.

Perhaps you too have buried the pain of a trauma, or experienced a period of intense stress as I had? It's worth examining your heart to find out.

CHAPTER 6

So, where was my pain?

The source of your pain will probably be quite different from mine, but if I tell you about mine you might see some similarities.

Firstly, it was to do with my mother's care. My mother lived with us for six years after my father died and most of the time it worked well. We were so used to people living with us that it did not seem difficult. She was the sixty-fifth person that we'd had to live with us in 50 years, and I was very glad to do it. In fact, it worked out brilliantly, as I grew closer to my mother than I'd ever been, and, as the time went on, I knew that she had prayed to invite Jesus into her heart. She enjoyed coming to church where people were very kind to her. A marvellous moment was when, prompted by one of the helpers that we had to stay with her when we went away, for the very first time in my life she was able to tell me with great difficulty that she loved me. I knew she loved me by her actions, my father was always the one who was free to say that he loved me, but she had actually never said it to me before.

Her care was manageable until she became very weak and kept falling, and the carers said that she was too frail and weak to climb the stairs anymore. This meant that we had to move her to a downstairs room which had limitations. There was only a toilet in that part of the house and no real washing facilities. It meant that I had occasionally to take my mother to a day centre to have a bath, which was not an easy task.

When we went out even for brief times, we never knew if she would be on the floor when we got back. She would never press the emergency button that we'd organised because she feared she'd be sent to hospital, so we had to arrange for someone to be there all the time which was never easy; and in itself became stressful. I was utterly exhausted by it all and knew that I could not continue.

I certainly did not want to put her into a care home, but the day came when that painful decision had to be made. Finding a place where she could be happy and be well cared for was no easy task. Over the next two years, she was in three different care homes. She had to leave the first one because after a bad fall they said that she needed nursing care, and they were not equipped to do that. I took her out of the second one because it was so horrible and she was so unhappy. It really upset me to see her there and I used to cry all the way home after each visit! In the third one, although it wasn't perfect, the staff were kind and tried to make life pleasant for her and keep her looking beautiful. Her complexion never faded, and her hair was always lovely.

On her 94th birthday my mother's Parkinson's meant she could not swallow solid food and so her cake was mixed with cream and given to her as a liquid. It was there in that home, a week before her 95th birthday that she died.... thankfully, to be with Jesus.

The whole issue with my mother was exhausting and agonising. By the time she died I had no tears left. I had done all my grieving whilst she was alive.

Have you had to care for someone else in this way?

Secondly, I knew that it was time to leave the church in Ely which we had pioneered in 1982. This was a very hard thing for me to consider. I felt we that couldn't leave until my mother wasn't coming to church anymore. It was the one highlight of her week and she had made some friends and was so happy to come with us.

Also, Tony was not convinced that we should leave, thinking I was just being emotional about the situation. That he wouldn't listen to me caused me frustration. To be fair, he was fairly distracted at the time by being a local councillor, finishing his time as chairman of the council, but he just wasn't prepared to consider it. I felt that I couldn't leave by myself. It was also important to me to be careful not to cause any difficulties in the church when we left. I wanted to protect what was now my son's ministry and the body of people that we loved; the church that we had given our lives for. It had to be done carefully and considerately.

However, despite knowing that it was the right thing to do, leaving the church was for me like experiencing a death or a divorce. It was the loss of many things. It meant leaving close fellowship with people whom we had loved, cared deeply for, visited, laughed with, cried with, prayed for, baptised, married and buried. Basically, dear friends, we had given our lives for the Church for 30 years! It felt part of us.

Have you experienced a loss too? With some it could be losing a job or a person, or when your children leave home or even your retirement. Loss takes many forms.

During this time, I was also very busy standing alongside Tony in his role of chairman of the district council. It meant going with him to many local events and always getting someone to be with my mother; which wasn't always easy. Mostly I enjoyed going with him as there were many opportunities to talk to people about the Lord. We also had the joy and privilege of going to a garden party at Buckingham Palace, but new hats and lovely outfits did not remove the stress!

A further complication after my mother went into care, was needing to sell the home we loved in Stuntney. For complicated reasons, we were struggling financially; and spiralling into debt. There was also the need to renovate parts of our property without the financial ability to do so. Tony was also experiencing greater weakness in his legs and problems with his balance. All of these things seemed to necessitate a move, and we eventually felt God was leading us to do it.

We had moved seven times in our married life, but this move was like no other I have ever experienced. This time, Tony was physically unable to do anything and there was no help available from our family, and for some inexplicable reason, almost no help from friends either until the very end. Consequently, the lot fell largely to me to pack and organise it almost single-handedly. For other moves, I had asked the removal people to pack for us, but as we were so short of money, I didn't feel able to pay the removal people to do the packing. This was a very bad decision!

Although we sold the house in just a few days, for almost the full asking price, complications with the dates and solicitors and removal men were horrendous, and most of the time I felt physically exhausted and often tempted to despair because nothing with the move seemed to go right. It didn't help either that we were in the midst of a breakdown of some of our family relationships, which was very painful indeed. No wonder I was in a terrible state by the time we got to Isleham and were settled in our new home. I was utterly broken in a way that I'd never been before.

What about your family? We all have some difficulties in our families! Have you too faced hard decisions? Have you felt you were struggling on your own with situations spiralling out of control?

When I looked back at my life, I felt rather puzzled, because in the past I had experienced very many hard things and remained buoyant. How could a divorce when I was young, and 25 years of ministry which was never easy, and a darling and much loved eight-year-old son's death not have the ability to break me, but all these things which had happened over a period of approximately two years did! However, I saw that all the troubles had come tumbling into my life at the same time, just like a tsunami!

Jesus said: *'Let not your heart be troubled.'* (John 14:1) Sadly however, I had let it be troubled. Then, I saw so clearly what had happened. All the traumas and resulting pain had knocked Jesus out of first place in my life. The issues had become bigger than Him. That was why I couldn't keep His peace in my heart, however hard I tried!

My faith had not gone, but it had lost its cutting edge. Some of it had been stolen! Maybe if I had been operating in overcoming faith I would never have been so distressed by all those things which happened. I began to pray and to surrender my pain to Him. After that I knew it could have no more power to harm me.

One day when I listened to the Lord and wrote down what He was saying. I said: *"Lord I'm looking for a great exchange… my pain for your comfort. Show me where you are and what you are doing Lord?"*

In my mind's eye, I immediately saw Him towering above every one of these difficult situations… He was so much bigger than all of them. I said to Him; *"Lord, I see you over all of it with your arms outstretched… completely enfolding every situation and every person involved in your arms. You are embracing everything!"*

He said to me; *"Trust me, press into my love for you and know that I have surrounded you with more love than you can ever imagine. You are rich in love and…..and I will keep it that way. Focus on me and who I am and who I have made you. Do not look to the right or to the left. Draw all the comfort that you need from Me because I am the source of all you need. Keep your eyes on My Word and every promise that I have given you and not on man's predictions. We will have supernatural results in all these situations because I have promised you My victory. I have laid out the way for you to receive it and I have provided the strength of many to ensure its delivery. BE STILL AND KNOW THAT I AM GOD!"*

Then I checked again whether there was anyone I needed to forgive; but what surprised me was that I needed to **forgive myself** for allowing it to happen at all!

Do you need to forgive yourself? Forgive friends, relations, authority figures? Whoever or whatever it is, your health depends on doing it.

Be sure to forgive anyone for anything and everything.

Then, as days went on, it suddenly dawned on me that all those difficulties I'd experienced were not simply due to natural reasons... It was *also* of course a **spiritual problem!**

Ephesians 6:12 tells us that '*we do not wrestle against flesh and blood, but against principalities, against powers, against the rulers of the darkness of this age, against spiritual hosts of wickedness in the heavenly places.*'

It goes on to instruct us to take up the whole armour of God that we may be able to withstand in the evil day, and having done all, to stand. It became clear that many things that had happened were due to a powerful demonic attack... forces that want to steal, kill and destroy!

I had taught this truth and lived this truth, but suddenly, as the revelation of it fell into my spirit afresh, strangely I felt so happy. I said to the Lord; "*That's IT Lord! Why didn't I **realise** that before?*"

He said to me… "*My child, there is nothing that I would not do for you. I treasure the purity of your heart greatly and I am working at keeping it so. You have now lifted your eyes higher to the truth that has set you free. My heart rejoices with your heart that has been cleansed and renewed in this area.*"

I had always tried hard not to apportion blame, but at that moment was wonderful to feel the complete release from **all temptation** to apportion blame. I felt a lightness of spirit and a wonderful new joy in my heart. No wonder God warns us in 1 Peter 5.8 to, '*be sober; be vigilant; because your adversary the devil walks about like a roaring lion, seeking whom he may devour.*' We must cooperate with God in not allowing him to devour us. I had nearly been devoured!

I have spent a lifetime pillaging from satan and I should have known that demonic manifestation is bound to arise when we are continually harassing him and taking back territory that he has stolen. But at that time, when I was so crushed and weary, I had not been as aware of that, nor as vigilant as I should have been. Of course, I was also hoping that God would bring good out of it all; even the nurse in the clinic had pointed out that possibility. God can always do that because He's a wonderful Redeemer; and He certainly did that when our son was killed in a road accident.

I journaled about how He could possibly turn all this to good and He said...

'*Do you see that it's our relationship that enables this to happen? It's relationship that makes the difference. Because you love me and you believe the best about me, I can turn all things round and make them work for your good. You have seen this at many times in your life. If you listed the 'bad' things that have happened to you, you would see that they were merely springboards for your advancement and things that worked compassion in you. You have those 'hind's feet' that enable you to have success on your high places of trouble, suffering and responsibility. I am not putting opposition in your life, but when it's there and you turn it over to me I'll do wonders that you've never dreamed of and lead you to victory in it and through it.*

'*You are My workmanship, you were so even before the foundation of the world – you were so before you were born– and I'm still fashioning you and making you in My image to be just like Me, just like the one who causes the sun to shine on the good and the evil.*

'As you keep your heart focused on Me and steadfast to Me – your heart is kept pure – and you leave Me free to do My work in others' lives. Judgement does not belong to you – love belongs to you and your life is enhanced by every moment that you allow My love to be pre-eminent in all things.'

Then, after dealing with the pain, God had instructed to cultivate joy. So, I looked on the internet for as many things as I could that would make me laugh. I found all sorts of things, like old television comedies, and television comedians on the internet and enjoyed them immensely. According to research, laughter increases blood flow, reduces pain, prevents disease, improves emotional health, and strengthens your spirit. In fact, I once read a story about a man who was healed simply by spending a lot of time laughing. For the sake of our health we must choose to laugh whether we feel like it or not.

The doctor was amazed that after the first treatment there was a 50% reduction of the lymphoma and after the next scan there was even less of it left. They told me this, but I also know because I saw the scans myself. So much for their doubts that the treatment could work well in a 73-year-old woman!

A tremendous highlight on my journey, occurred just before the fifth treatment. I was visited by Dan, my pastor friend who is now an evangelist with "Through Faith Missions". He called in to see me on his way to a Prayer for Parliament meeting London. When he arrived, we all began to worship the Lord together. As we did so, he anointed me with oil and prayed. Immediately, I felt an extraordinary rush of power, like a wind blowing through me. It was like cleansing tide and at that moment, I knew beyond all doubt that whatever was left of the cancer had gone.

I nearly didn't get to the fifth treatment because it snowed heavily, and the roads were terrible. A friend rang me and said roads were blocked. Could I change the date? Well no, that's just impossible! As we left Isleham the snow plough was clearing ahead of us, but as fast as it cleared the road, the wind was blowing the snow back onto the road.

As I had believed that the lymphoma had now completely left my body, that day I was eager to get to the examination with the consultant. I prayed that we'd make it!

After I'd had the usual blood tests, the weighing and measuring, I met the consultant for my pre-treatment examination. They always want to make sure that you are well enough to take the treatment, but this time I was very surprised at how thoroughly the consultant examined me, far more thoroughly than any of the others had on other days. Looking puzzled he checked and double-checked my body.

To start with I didn't tell him what I thought had happened to me in the time of prayer, but when he had carefully palpated all the places where the lymph nodes were previously enlarged and sick and he said; *"I can find nothing!"*

I told him; *"That's because it's gone!"* I explained that we had prayed and that I had felt the remainder of the cancer leave my body! I told him that I knew that it had gone! This is the moment when often medical people's eyes glaze over and a sweet tolerating smile comes to the unbelieving face! At least he didn't say anything negative!

As I'm writing this a thought occurred to me for the first time. Why didn't I say to the consultant that I wanted a scan because I believed that the cancer had gone? Why didn't I call a halt to the treatment right then?

In hindsight it would have seemed the right thing to do, but at the time I didn't even consider it for more than a fleeting second. I had committed to the six treatments and that was that!

Then, the story came to my mind in 2 Kings 13 where Elisha was approached by the kings for help. The king was instructed to shoot an arrow as far as he could, then to take the rest of the arrows and strike the ground. When he only struck the ground three times Elisha was disappointed. He said, *'you should have struck the ground five or six times!'*(v19)

I thought... Ah! Like the king I need to strike this thing enough times to be totally sure that it is gone! When I was sharing this with someone else, they confirmed that by saying; *"Maybe God was using those extra treatments to make doubly sure that it never came back."* Maybe I'll never know.

As I daily soaked myself in the Word, I was led to the passage in Exodus where God promised Israel that it would be **His hand** that would deliver them. I had also heard this preached many years previously and was able to find the YouTube sermon by Jerry Savelle quite easily, which I listened to several times.

The revelation God was imparting to me was clear: the hand of the Lord had delivered Israel from Egypt; His hand had brought judgement on their enemies but blessing upon Israel.

Just as with Israel, I knew that the hand of the Lord would be upon me, to bless me and deliver me, and upon my enemies (cancer cells) to destroy them. *'And the Egyptians shall know that I am the* Lord, *when I stretch out My hand on Egypt and bring out the children of Israel from among them.'* Exodus 7:5

I saw the chemo as the vengeance of God working against the enemy. It was the power of His right hand saving me. '*Though I walk in the midst of trouble, You will revive me; You will stretch out Your hand against the wrath of my enemies, and Your right hand will save me.*' Psalm 138:7

I thought a lot about the personal application of three healing Scriptures. Firstly:

'*Surely, He has borne our griefs and carried our sorrows; yet we esteemed Him stricken, smitten by God, and afflicted. But He was wounded for our transgressions, He was bruised for our iniquities; the chastisement for our peace was upon Him, and by His stripes we are healed.*' Isaiah 53:4-5

Secondly, Scripture says about Jesus:

'*Who Himself bore our sins in His own body on the tree, that we, having died to sins, might live for righteousness—by whose stripes you were healed.*' 1 Peter 2:24

Thirdly Acts 10:38 says:

'*How God anointed Jesus of Nazareth with the Holy Spirit and with power, who went about doing good and healing all who were oppressed by the devil, for God was with Him.*'

I often said quietly to myself as I focused on the Lord, sometimes seeing Him on the cross and other times just in front of me; '*Jesus, you personally bore my sins and my sickness in your body on the tree and by your stripes I was healed. Thank you for healing me.*'

Knowing He's done all that is necessary to make the gift of healing available to me by His work on the cross, I could reach out and receive my healing by faith, and I could take it boldly!

CHAPTER 7

How can we co-operate with God?

The first thing we can do is to be sure that we have given God full access to our life is by inviting Him and His Holy Spirit into our hearts, totally yielding ourselves to Him.

You may just have read that account and thought... *'Well, I want God in my life, and I do sort of know God, and I go to church. I am a believer… but I don't think I feel about God the way Margaret does.'*

So, my question is: Do you know that you're born again and are you filled with his Holy Spirit? If you don't know or you are not sure, then why not take a moment and pray this prayer with me...

Dear God,

I come to you in the name of Jesus, and I want to make a choice about my life. I believe that Jesus died for me on the cross, shed His blood to wash away my sins, and rose from the dead enabling me to reconnect with the Father.

Thank you that His act of love paid the price for me to have fellowship with you, and to live eternally with you.

So, Heavenly Father, I repent, by turning my back on the life that I have lived without you. I repent of the things in my life which have grieved you.

I don't want to follow you half-heartedly anymore, and today, I choose to follow You Jesus, wholeheartedly from this moment on.

I ask you, Jesus, to be the Lord of my life and to come and live within me. I want to worship you in spirit and in truth and I will tell others about your love.

Because I have made this sincere connection with you, I believe that I am born again. My spirit is a new creation, and I stand before you, heavenly father forgiven, because Jesus Himself paid the price for my sin. Thank you for loving me.

Now there is one more step you can take. You can receive the Baptism of the Holy Spirit. Simply pray the following...

Now, Jesus, will you baptise me into your Holy Spirit; will you fill me full to overflowing with Yourself.

Let me praise you in my own language and also, Lord, let me praise you in a new language beyond the limitations of my intellect. Thank you that because I am baptised into your Holy Spirit I can speak in tongues. I know that I am now able to speak in a language that you give me, that I don't understand, but I know that your Word says that you hear me and understand me. Thank you because you say that this language will empower me and strengthen me and enable me to feel close to You. Give me the words, Lord, and I will speak them.

In the name of Jesus, amen.

Now take a few moments to worship Him, expecting Him to give you a heavenly language; and if it doesn't happen right now, expect it in the days to come. Remember that the Scripture says: '*and **they** were filled with the **Holy Spirit** and began to speak with other tongues, as the Spirit gave them utterance.*' Acts 2.4

Meaning: They began to speak as the Holy Spirit gave them His words!

When you feel the words of the Spirit bubbling up, speak forth and remember, God won't force you; you must decide to say those words even if they sound strange.

Now you can build your faith!

I am very blessed that I did not have to start building my faith from scratch. For over 40 years I had lived in the Bible. I had read it right through over 20 times, I had made a practice of meditating on the Word and have loved the Word of God dearly. I truly had its treasure hidden in my heart.

However, recently I felt moved to re-read the first book which inspired me to live by faith; '*Realities*' *by Basilea Schlink*, and I wept copiously when I realised how, through succumbing to the weariness of a time of trial, I had actually lost the cutting edge of my faith. Something did need to be regained and rebuilt. However, I was working on it; and in this crisis situation I was now fully focused on His promises; and ready to go to battle with them!

There are lots of ways that you too can build your faith. Part of that is having right biblical beliefs such as understanding who the real author of sickness is.

Most of all… Don't blame God!

Recently I was talking to two separate people who each blamed God for the death of someone precious to them and were angry with Him. One said to me; "*God took my son!*" And; "*God took my husband!* "Consequently, all their trust in Him had gone.

People often have the idea when things go wrong, because they believe that God is sovereign, if He decides to take someone, He will do so. However, I don't believe He is deciding at whim to take people to heaven or send them to hell. I believe that He does act sovereignly… but… He always acts according to His Word.

The worst phrase I've heard in connection with this idea is: "*Well, God needed Him in heaven more than we needed him on earth!*" What rubbish that is! If the person was a fervent Christian, God needs them here to get people healed and saved, not enjoying heaven. The problem is that it's much easier to blame God for your problems rather than take responsibility either for a corrupt or mismanaged lifestyle, or to find out from God's word what he really thinks and what He really wants to do.

Another thing is that people read the Old Testament, and it seems to say that God put sickness on people. Whatever it says in the Old Testament… we don't live in that dispensation, we live in the New Testament era, in the era **after** the cross: **which changed everything!**

When my son died in a road accident, people tried to tell me that God had taken my son. It troubled me when people said that because I knew that was wrong. How could they say that about my loving heavenly Father? Later I found out that it was wrong, because Scripture says two things:

Firstly that, *Children are a gift from God* and secondly that *the gifts and callings of God are without repentance.* God doesn't give a child and then take it away despite the popular Christian song that says so, and despite those words which are spoken in the Anglican funeral service.

God gives generously and certainly doesn't take away children. If He were to ask us to relinquish something it would only be because he had something much better in mind for us. It is satan who is the thief that comes to steal, kill and destroy. I told those people, who were saying God had taken my son, that if my earthly father had 'taken' or killed my son then we would have put him in prison!

God is certainly not a thief; satan is the thief. Jesus tells us that His Father is a most wonderful loving heavenly Father. He is not the same as any other father; any imperfect earthly father. God is never our **problem,** He is always the **answer** and although we don't see everyone healed, Scripture tells us that Jesus never refused to heal anyone who came to Him. He is the giver of good gifts.

Jesus assures us that If we ask for bread, His father won't give us a stone. If we ask for fish, He won't give us a snake, because; *'Every good gift and every perfect gift are from above, and comes down from the Father of lights, with whom there is no variation or shadow of turning.'* James 1:17

In Exodus 15.23 the father revealed one of his covenant names. He said: *am the Lord your healer. I am Jehovah Rapha.* This is how the Father revealed Himself in the Old Testament and He sent Jesus to give us more revelation of who He is. Jesus is just like the Father. *'He is **the image of the invisible God,** the firstborn over all creation.'* Colossians 1:15

When Philip asked Jesus what the Father was like: *'Have I been with you so long and yet you have not known Me, Philip? He who has seen Me has seen the Father; so how can you say, 'Show us the Father'?* John 14:9

Take note what Jesus said, "If you've seen Me you've seen the Father!" The Jesus I read about in the Bible and know, was angry with the hypocrites and those peddling dead religion, but He showed overwhelming compassion to the sinner and the sick person. Six times it says...**He healed them all.**

So, if '*He is the same yesterday today* and *forever*' as Hebrews 13.8 says. He is still the Lord our healer and it's is not just His name; it's who He is through and through.

So, why would He not heal me? Why would He not want to heal you? Why would He not have compassion on you and me just as He had compassion on those He met during His life on earth?

Some examples of those healings:

Then His fame went throughout all Syria; and they brought to Him all sick people who were afflicted with various diseases and torments, and those who were demon-possessed, epileptics, and paralytics; and He healed them.' Matthew 4:24

'*When the sun was setting, all those who had any that were sick with various diseases brought them to Him; and He laid His hands on every one of them and healed them.*' Luke 4:4

'*And the whole multitude sought to touch Him, for power went out from Him and healed them all.*' Luke 6:19

I particularly love the passage where the leper comes to him and says; "*If You are willing, You can make me clean.*"

'*Then Jesus, moved with compassion, stretched out His hand and touched him, and said to him, "I am willing; be cleansed.*" Mark 1:40-41

Note that He said, "*I AM WILLING!*"

There is no doubt in my mind that just as He was willing to heal me, He is willing to heal the one who is reading this story. He is no respecter of persons, and if you ask Him and if you can receive it from Him by faith.... He is willing! He wants to heal!

We never need to pray for healing saying '*if it be your will*' as Jesus did in the garden of Gethsemane. We would only do that when we have a need for direction in life. If it is Your will that I do this or that? We can easily know the will of the Father, by watching what Jesus did, because as we look at Him, **we will see the Father's will being carried out by His obedient son.**

So, if God is not the author of sickness, who is?

We must be utterly convinced that God is not the author of sickness, but that it is a tool of God's enemy satan. Sickness came into the world when satan tempted Adam to sin. However, sickness is not necessarily due to our own sin , but Is there because we live in a fallen world.

There are lies that even some Christians believe about sickness. Some believe that its a blessing in disguise, or that God has put it on us, or even allowed it to come upon us to teach us something or to punish us.

We must be utterly sure in our own hearts that these ideas are lies. If we believe them they undermine our faith and cancel our ability to receive healing.

Is it ever our fault that we are sick?

Well, it might be…by default. We might have let it in without realising it… certainly if we smoke, we can invite sickness. If we eat a rubbish diet, we can allow it to take hold of us. But saying that we allowed it, is not the same as it being put upon us by God. The best is that even if it was our fault, it wouldn't stop Him having compassion on us and healing us , as long as we get rid of any guilt attached to that. This is when repentance can be the gateway to life. All we have to do is to come to Him, make that decision to change what we did and what we think and receive the healing balm of His forgiveness. He paid a great price with His death on the cross to make this available to us.

When we understand who is really to blame for our problem, we can use the authority that Christ has given us to send him packing! The Bible shows us clearly how we are to resist the devil and sickness. We do this by yielding to God and using the name of Jesus.

James 4:7 says: '*Therefore, submit to God. <u>Resist the devil</u> and he will flee from you.*'

If you don't understand how to do this, do find someone who does know how to pray against our enemy the devil, with faith and power.

CHAPTER 8
Indispensable beliefs that build faith

Knowing who we are in Christ, is a vital and indispensable belief!

There are certain key beliefs that really help us to have faith in God.

But nothing builds faith like knowing who God says we are. We don't have to worry about what anyone else says if we know what He says about us. But we need to decide to believe that we are who He says we are. When I'm secure in my identity I can live my life in Him confidently.

For instance;

I know that through the blood of the cross I've been made righteous. I'm a new creation reborn in His image… the old Margaret has passed away.

I'm established, anointed and sealed by God's Holy Spirit.

I'm seated with Him in heavenly places, far above all principalities and powers.

I'm God's co-worker, I am loved, I am accepted.

I'm Jesus' friend, I have been given His authority; I am one spirit with Him.

I'm a joint heir with Jesus and I am complete in Him.

Whoopee! that's so wonderful! And if you are saved… its true of you too! This is YOUR identity!

I can find many other statements from the Word of God that show us our new identity in HIM… and we need to build these wonderful statements of the truth into our hearts. Meditate on them until we have it written in our hearts forever. Doesn't God promise that the law would no longer be given to us on tablets of stone but that he would write his law in our hearts?

Over the years I have also come to believe in my heart that without any doubt I am a beloved child of God, whom God loves as much as He loves His son Jesus. I know that God loves me unconditionally, and I have experienced this wonderful love since I was saved in 1973, in good times and in bad times, especially in the bad times!

Now, if we know that we are children of God, we too can be sure that He is a wonderful daddy, the daddy who has put healing on the table for us all.

Jesus made that clear when He spoke to a Syrophoenician woman in the Bible whom he knew didn't have a covenant with God. In the remarks He makes to her, He assures us that Healing belongs to God's children. He says:

Healing is the children's bread! Bread was not a luxury or an extra in those days; it was a basic necessity for life.

So, guess what? If it's true that I'm a beloved child of God, born of God, born of His Spirit, **as you are too** if you are a Christian… we are part of his family; we are forever joined to HIM FOR ETERNITY. This of course means that we are joint heirs with Him, and as a joint heir, **ALL** that the Father has belongs to me!

This is such an enormous truth, sometimes hard to believe; but if we ask Him, God will give us this amazing revelation that will give us great strength to endure and overcome all things.

The result of knowing all of this means that we can rejoice and delight in who we are in Him. We can come to Him with childlike faith simply trusting our amazing Father with our requests. Then will He not delight to fulfil our requests? I believe He will.

Meditate on these truths, because the sure knowledge of your acceptance, your position in Him, and particularly your sonship, is a big start to finding victory.

Know you have been made worthy!

I believe that many Christians don't receive healing because they feel unworthy. Of course, to believe that we are unworthy is a lie of the devil, who has used life's events and problems to convince us. Despite it being wrong, that's just how some people feel. I have seen that these strong feelings can put a barrier up which keeps God's healing out. People can think.... if He really knew me; if He really knew what I was like.... He couldn't love me, and certainly wouldn't heal me.

But the truth is that God does know ALL about us. Nothing is hidden from Him. He knows us intimately and understands us completely. Doesn't this make His unconditional love and care for us utterly remarkable?

This idea that He can't heal us because we are unworthy does not stand up when we look at the evidence of Scripture. Let us look at the stories of Jesus healing people. Six times the Bible says that he healed *a multitude*...and that He healed ***them all*** because He had compassion on them!

Don't you think that somewhere in that multitude there would have been a few folks that maybe we could have considered unworthy to receive the healing? Of course, there were…. but they all *did receive it*. Not **one** was left sick, even those whom we might have considered unworthy!

Why is it utterly wrong for a Christian to consider himself unworthy? It's because Jesus by His sacrifice on the cross made us the righteousness of God in Him. **He** has made us worthy. He paid an enormous price to accomplish this. Let's honour His sacrifice.

Believe the truth of God's Word!

If you have not really believed that the word of God is true and reliable, this is the moment to decide to do it.

The Word of God is so precious to me. It has been a rock in my life, a source of tremendous inspiration. I love Proverbs 4:20 which says; *'My son, give attention to my words; incline your ear to my sayings. Do not let them depart from your eyes; Keep them in the midst of your heart; they are life to those who find them, and health to all their flesh. Keep your heart with all diligence, for out of it spring the issues of life. Put away from you a deceitful mouth and put perverse lips far from you.'*

When it says '**they**', it is talking about His words. His words are LIFE to those that **find** them; there's actual life in them: spiritual life and physical life; as we believe them and truly take them into our hearts. This is more than just having them in our minds; it is when we have taken time to put them into the deep places of our heart, that they become effective.

I have not always believed His word like that. In 1964, I was twenty years old, and in Greece on a student holiday when the idea first struck me that the Word of God could be true rather than a whole load of stories made up by someone. As we stood In Athens on Mars

Hill looking towards The Acropolis, the secular tour guide said; "*This is where St Paul stood and preached the Gospel.*"

This statement fell into my heart and light began to shine with a completely new revelation. I was stunned. I thought, '*So Paul was a real man, who was really here and really preached the gospel! WOW... then... maybe the Bible is TRUE.*'

Astounding as it may seem, as a lifelong churchgoer, I had never considered that the Bible was actually true.

However, now that I was diagnosed with a life-threatening disease, I was so grateful that I already fully understood the blessings of paying attention to His Word and of hiding it in my heart.

Meditating on the Word increases faith!

I knew that meditating on the Word of God was a powerful way of increasing my faith and also a powerful way of controlling my thoughts, so that I don't speak negative things over myself... This is what the Bible calls, 'a deceitful mouth.' If we maintain our gaze upon the natural circumstances, we can easily waver; but if we keep our eyes fixed on the healing promises in His Word, we can keep our hearts steady because the Word never changes: it's always positive.

The Word tells us in 2 Corinthians 4:16-18**...**

'*Therefore, do not lose heart. Even though our outward man is perishing, yet the inward man is being renewed day by day. For our light affliction, which is but for a moment, is working for us a far more exceeding and eternal weight of glory, while we do not look at the things which are seen, but at the things which are not seen. For the things which are seen are temporary, but the things which are not seen are eternal.*'

so we are **not** to fix our eyes on our sickness or on things in the world which are temporary and are always changing. In this Scripture, Paul calls them light *afflictions*, although they may not feel like it at the time (mine certainly didn't). Of course, in the light of eternity, these last only for a moment, and can actually work something good in us. So, Paul tells us; instead of looking at those unreliable changing things, we are to look at things which are unseen and eternal. His word fills that bill.

I believe that the word of God is eternal and true and powerful, and that I can rely on it. I can have confidence in it. I can believe that He will do what it says He will do.

'For as the rain comes down, and the snow from heaven, and do not return there, but water the earth, and make it bring forth and bud, that it may give seed to the sower and bread to the eater, So shall My word be that goes forth from My mouth; It shall not return to Me void, But it shall accomplish what I please, And it shall prosper in the thing for which I sent it.' Isaiah 55:10-11

God has sent His Word into the earth just like He has sent the rain to water the earth. When the earth receives the water, it causes life to come in the earth. When the Word of God comes into our hearts, it has the power to give birth to whatever it says.

There is such power in returning His word to Him… and how we can do that is by speaking it out… declaring it… and agreeing with it. He says to "put Him in remembrance of it"; or REMIND Him of what He has said.

He says: *'My covenant I will not break, nor alter the word that has gone out of My lips.'* Psalm 89:34

How reassuring that when God has made a covenant, His promise is that He will never break it! The whole Bible is based on covenant, blood covenant, which historically is a completely unbreakable agreement. Once God has said something. That's IT! We can *'watch this space'* for it to come to pass.

Some of the greatest promises in Scripture, prophesied in the Old Testament, enable me to believe that His word is true. For instance, God promised in the Old Testament that Israel, God's people, would be brought back to their own land, and that the desert would blossom like a rose. This has happened! He promised the Jews their messiah and foretold the birth of Jesus, in detail, right through the Old Testament; and it certainly came true. So many of the prophecies in the Old Testament have come true, and some of it has actually happened in my lifetime! So we can clearly see, by this very evident fulfilment, that God's word is true and that He is faithful to it.

So many prophecies and scriptures in the Bible promise healing, and so we can consider with faith, Romans 8.32; *'He who did not spare His own son – but gave Him up for us all– will He not also along with Him graciously give us ALL THINGS.'*

If He was prepared to give His own son, will He not give us ALL THINGS WITH HIM? Yes, He will! I know that the Word of God has a clear message, both in the New Testament and the Old Testament; that it is God's will to heal us. I have been wonderfully healed and seen others healed too many times to doubt it.

Believe in His compassion

Even in just a couple of verses of Matthew, it's clear that healing is ours… because of His compassion.

In Matthew 14:13, even when Jesus was trying to get away from the crowd, when they found Him, it says that **His heart was moved with compassion** for them and He healed all of them.

Again, later in the chapter in verse 36, it says that everyone who touched Him was instantly healed. We just have to touch Him, even the hem of His garment as the woman with the issue of blood did.

I love the way The Passion translation of the Bible reveals what the result of our healing will be in Matthew 15.31; '*For three days everyone celebrated the miracles, as they exalted and praised the God of Israel!*' (TPT). Simply put, Jesus has compassion on the sick, Jesus turns nobody away and God is glorified, and will be glorified by our healing. So let's have the faith of the woman with the issue of blood… if we but touch the hem of His garment with our faith, we can be healed.

Healing is already provided

I truly believed that God had already provided all I needed to be made completely well, by His work on the cross, so I knew that all I needed to do was get into a position to receive it. One preacher whom I heard said; "*You have to get under the spout where the glory comes out!*" God encourages us to ask Him to heal us; but He doesn't tell us we have to beg Him for it. We just have to receive what he has already provided.

In fact, people asked why I'd called my Facebook page '*Margaret's Journey to Health*' and not '*Margaret's Journey to Healing.*' It's because in spiritual terms, it's all done. If I'm saved, then I'm already healed! The Greek word sozo, which is translated "saved", includes healing! But I had not yet regained complete health. Some people were surprised how positive I was; but bearing in mind my knowledge of God and His Word and my previous experiences, it would have been more surprising to me if I had not been positive.

CHAPTER 9

Spiritual support and human support...

In these serious times of sickness, as you wait for your healing to manifest you must find human support as well as spiritual support. You need a small group of people or someone who will be positive and encourage you. I certainly knew that I was not alone; a few close friends were often there for me: and because I've lived a fairly public life and have been involved with so many people, a much larger group cheered from the side-lines.

Many people instantly responded to an *accidental admission* that I had cancer on a friend's Facebook page. I had forgotten how public a post can be… my friend was talking about having cancer and all I said was… "me too!" The response came immediately; "*Margaret: do you have cancer?*" Once I had admitted it, the reaction came from far and wide; literally from all over the world, and it came like a tsunami. Once it was '*out,*' I made a Facebook page called '*Margaret's Journey to Health.*' After that I knew that very many people were all rooting for me, and best of all, praying with faith.

What a mixed bunch of people responded. There were people of amazing stature who had ministered in our church over the years; there were also people whom I'd ministered to, particularly those whom I had personally supported through their own experience with cancer. There were close as well as distant friends. There were people who had been part of our congregation and other people whom I'd blessed in some way. I treasured each one of them. God showed me that this amazing response was in fact a harvest: that for years I'd sown for it, and now it was time to reap.

I was so blessed to be surrounded by so many positive and supportive people. The church where we are currently was a wonderful loving support to us.
When our friend Rod Anderson and his wife Julie came to pray with me, he was very fierce about not allowing anyone through the door who could speak negatively into my life! I could honestly say that I did not have anyone who came to see me who spoke negatively. What a wonderful thing to be able to say!

My husband Tony was, of course, an amazing support. Nothing seemed too much trouble for him. His patience seemed everlasting, and his prayers and love were very evident and available to me. I often felt concerned about him as it is no mean feat to become the carer of someone helpless at the age of 78. Words cannot express how deeply grateful I am to have a loving, caring, Godly husband in my life, who I'm still in love with after over 50 years.

Neither can words adequately express how thankful I am for all the support that was given to me by so many others, which was practical as well as spiritual. People strengthened me by sending Bible-based declarations, prayers, Scriptures, and videos. Never underestimate the power of loving notes if you know someone who is ill.

Many people from the church here in Isleham and my previous church in Ely to visit me. They came to pray for me, to clean the house and many brought delicious meals. People drove from as far away as Doncaster, Hunstanton and London. It made me smile to think that I had gone all the way to California, and Turkey, to comfort a friend in their time of need.

One especially precious time of prayer was when I sat on my sofa with two ladies, Pauline and Tracey. Pauline had previously had bladder cancer, but didn't have medical treatment: she had taken the alternative route and was healed; Tracey had the medical treatment for her breast cancer and was healed. Then one precious day there they were sitting either side of me praying! They said: "*You supported us and now it's your turn*! I was much moved.

Here are some of the amazing messages I was sent:

Alison sent me this precious message; "*The prayers you have prayed for healing for others are like the garments Dorcas made. I saw God holding them up. Knowing that God hears our prayers, I will be praying and fasting for you tomorrow.*"

Michelle sent this message based on Scripture; '*Margaret will not despair because she believes that she will see the goodness of the Lord in the land of the living. Right here and now she will wait for and confidently expect the Lord. She is strong and takes courage. Yes, she will confidently wait and expect the Lord.*'

Lizzie sent Isaiah 58.8; '*Then shall your light break forth as the morning and thine health shall spring forth speedily, and thy righteousness shall go before thee and the glory of the Lord shall be your rear-guard.*'

Ann-Marie sent this; "*I totally believe that we shall see the full manifestation of Margaret's healing – this battle was fought over 2000 years ago so whatever route you take, it will not change the outcome. **Margaret is healed**! I am praying for the manifestation in Margaret's body to line up with that truth!*"

Doreen sent this... '*Hello, my sweet girl - do you not know that you are not your own but you have been bought with a price and that you are now in Christ, so this disease is illegal. It must go! We learn of Jehovah*

Rapha... the Lord our healer, who heals all our disease. Praying and waiting for this manifestation of God as He promised when we agree!"

How precious that a dear young man called Jon sent me Psalm 103, which he said that he had prayed for himself every day since I had ministered to him years ago when he was ill!: *'Bless the LORD, O my soul; and all that is within me, bless His holy name! Bless the LORD, O my soul ,and forget not all His benefits: Who forgives all your iniquities, Who heals all your diseases, Who redeems your life from destruction, who crowns you with lovingkindness and tender mercies, Who satisfies your mouth with good things, So that your youth is renewed like the eagle's.'*

Tracey said; *"Those who leave everything in God's hands will eventually see God's hand in everything Looking forward to your complete healing and looking back to see how He has worked through you Margaret, and reached many with your joy, love and courage."*

Flowers and gifts came constantly, with cards and loving notes. One friend, Yvonne, sent a bag of seven prettily wrapped gifts with the instruction to open one a day: they were such delightful little gifts which included Vera Lynn's life story; so entertaining and easy to read.

Later, because she's an expert in sugar craft, she sent a little sugar craft duck dressed in wellingtons that she had made for me. It was so cute! We also had an unexpected visit from her husband, who was a delivery man for Tesco, and one day happened to deliver our order.

Another friend, Wendy, sent me the most beautiful knitted dolly which she had made herself which she had prayed over and soaked with fragrant anointing oil. The dolly's name was Summer. I thought it was a prophetic name as I expected my natural and my spiritual summer after a terrible winter. One person thought it very strange when I told them I'd been sent a doll, but that doll gave me enormous joy and special comfort. I'm not ashamed to say that I often hugged it as I went to sleep, smelling that wonderful perfumed oil that Wendy had soaked her with.

These words and gifts were such a great encouragement to me. I used them to fuel my faith and keep my heart secure in God, wrote them all down in my book, and read them often. What a wonderful heart-warming harvest! I could honestly say that I had poured out my life unstintingly for others for so many years and it seemed that God was returning the gift. It seemed as if it was truly; '...*pressed down, shaken together and running over.*' Luke 6:38

But, you might say... if you are taking the treatments, why would take such intense steps to keep the Word in your heart?

The encouragement that my friend Rebecca sent me as I was praying what to do, highlighted the reason for this: '*Your trust in Him counts beyond the means itself.*'

Faith lifts everything into a new dimension and even causes the medical treatment to be more effective.

I encourage you ...to Fill your heart with the Word, day, and night!

Its good if we have established our hearts with Biblical truth about healing long before we get sick! But... If you are not there yet, it is definitely not too late! If you are starting from scratch, you can begin to fill your heart with God's truth about healing.

I took every single word that people gave me, every scripture that was highlighted to me by the Holy Spirit and every prophetic word that I had been given and wrote them in an exercise book. I treasured them. I had done this for many years, but I knew that this was definitely the time to start another little book!

'My son, give attention to my words; incline your ear to my sayings. Do not let them depart from your eyes; Keep them in the midst of your heart; for they are life to those who find them, And health to all their flesh. Keep your heart with all diligence, for out of it spring the issues of life.'
Proverbs 4:20-24

Or again in Psalm 1:1-3 it says *'Blessed is the man who walks not in the counsel of the ungodly, nor stands in the path of sinners, nor sits in the seat of the scornful; But his delight is in the law of the LORD, AND in His law he meditates day and night. He shall be like a tree planted by the rivers of water that brings forth its fruit in its season, whose leaf also shall no wither; and whatever he does shall prosper.'*

God's truth has to become our **own** truth not just what someone else has said. It has to be planted in our own hearts; then we will be in a place where we actively expect God to move on our behalf.

Do you have any prophetic words that you can use to strengthen your faith?

In 1 Timothy 1:18; we find: *according to the prophecies previously made concerning you, that by them you may wage the good warfare.* We can wage warfare by meditating on these prophecies and keeping them alive in our hearts. They are purveyors of hope and builders of faith. I knew that I had unfulfilled prophecy on my life. I knew that I had a strong hope for the future.

'For I know the plans and thoughts that I have for you,' says the LORD, 'plans for peace and well-being and not for disaster, to give you a future and a hope.' Jeremiah 29:11

Here are some of the prophetic words that I treasured:

One wonderful prophetic word I was given at Bethel in March 2017 was this:

"I see you on a horse riding through meadows and fields at a fast pace with the wind whipping through your hair. God had given you a high-speed adventure where he will show you the wonders of his love and His assignment for the next season of your life. There is no fear in this lovely adventure. I see you with your face to the sky adorning Him as he looks down and adored you too. Oh, what a beautiful love you both have for each other. I see an old-fashioned alarm clock and the Lord wants you to know that your time isn't over. You have a lot of living still to do. He is renewing your youth. He still has assignments for you, precious daughter."

This word is so interesting, because, without realising it, in 2017, I must have already been sick when He gave it to me.

A friend called Barbara had sent this prophecy in 2013:

"Get ready to gird up your loins. It is time to outrun the chariots. (1 Kings 18:46) *There are still unfulfilled promises on your lives. God is about to turn things around and open doors for you that you never expect to be opened and pour out such blessing that you will not have room to contain it. Hold fast to the promise of God.* Hebrews 10:35. *The Lord says that the latter days of Tony and Margaret are more than at the beginning.* (Job 42:12)

Then Sharon Stone gave me this prophecy, also in 2017 at a meeting in Huntingdon; *"Father, I ask you to bless Margaret – right now in the name of Jesus. The spirit of the Lord says: daughter I have always made you a builder of my family even from the time that you were young. You were the one who had an anointing to build the family of God and to build faith. But also, you are a repairer of the breach and one that was **known for** giving others fresh start and new beginnings. Then I transitioned you to a place where you were a raiser of leaders. There are churches that exist today because of the leaders that you have raised and there are lives that were broken that are whole because of what you have done. The strategy that I am operating in your life now is different. Do not look on an official* *network of who is on a membership, or who is associated with a stream. See it as how I am connecting my body. There is an apostolic anointing on you that helps launch ministers and ministries into the next phase of their ministry when they get stuck. I am releasing a sending anointing upon you that you might be sent forth to create a momentum to unstick churches and ministers, that they might be mobilised to the next dimension There will be some who rejoice to see you come and others that rejoice to see you go. Know this; change at times has to be forced."*

On the 9th August 2017 in Hunstanton, Dan said; *"The next three years of your ministry will be the most anointed of your whole life bringing great fruit into being."*

You can see that by these prophetic words, God was encouraging me, whatever it looked like in my life, not to give up or throw in the towel. He was definitely encouraging me to look ahead and believe for a great future.

At the time I received them I had no idea how much I would need to pay attention to those words.

God has a very personal word for you

I encourage you to ask the Lord for a special Scripture which He can speak into your heart and use to quicken your faith.

I had many Scriptures that built my faith, but as I sought Him at that time, the most significant Scripture that God highlighted to me was Deuteronomy 33:27; *"The eternal God is your refuge, and underneath are the everlasting arms; He will thrust out the enemy from before you, and will say, 'Destroy!'"* All through the time of sickness, I would use this scripture to speak to the Lymphoma. Especially during chemo sessions, I would say quietly to myself with a smile; *"God Himself is destroying you!"* I believe that this is just what happened! God destroyed it!

I often said quietly to myself as I focused on the Lord, sometimes seeing Him on the cross and other times just in front of me; *'Jesus, you personally bore my sins and my sickness in your body on the tree and by your stripes I was healed. Thank you for healing me.'*

Knowing He's done all that is necessary to make the gift of healing available to me, by His work on the cross, I could reach out and receive my healing by faith, and I could take it boldly! What Jesus did on the cross, we can understand as a **finished work**, because He has made everything available to us already. Forgiveness for our sins, healing for our bodies, provision for our earthly needs.

CHAPTER 10
Relationship: The key to confidence!

A close relationship with God is a big key to being confident that we will receive what we ask from Him. It's so important to confess God's Word, but confessing God's Word without relationship can just be empty words. Day by day we can develop relationship with Him by spending time in His presence, and through that giving Him access to our heart and mind. We need to develop a life-giving intimacy with Jesus through the Holy Spirit. When we have that intimacy with Him, it's easy to take His promises for ourselves personally. In the times when I just soaked in His presence, I thought about the Scripture from the Song of Solomon 6:3; '*I am my beloved's and He is mine.*' and I would mutter it to myself.

Realising the depth of belonging we have with Jesus is so important, it's a symbiosis – a supernatural union that Jesus says causes fruit to be born. Out of intimacy with Him, supernatural life comes!

In other words, because I knew Him, and knew His word, and I knew His will, I could let His words find their home in me. I could relax, I could trust in Him completely, knowing that whatever I had the faith to ask Him for, He would do. It is abiding in Him that brings strong expectation for His personal intervention.

'*If **you** abide in Me, and My words abide in you, you will ask what you desire, and it shall be done for you.*' John 15:7

In November, a month after starting the treatment, God clearly gave a promise to me from Psalm 91; '***Because I have set my love upon Him,*** *He will deliver me. He will set me on high because I have known His name. I will call upon Him and He will answer me. He will be with me in trouble. He will deliver me and honour me. With long life he will satisfy me and show me His salvation.*'

I knew that I had set my love upon HIM and I had known His name. I knew He was with me in trouble and I knew He would deliver me and honour me; so it's only a small step to believe that with long life, He will satisfy me and show me His salvation!

Know for certain that as we personally draw close to Him, acknowledge His presence, enjoy His presence, have faith in His presence, we build our faith, and healing will come out of that relationship. In that relationship we can bask in His love and enjoy His love for us.

The greatest lie we can believe is that because things have '*gone wrong,*' because bad things are happening to us, that He doesn't love us anymore. Paul had more trouble than any other disciple recorded in the Bible. He had the most tremendous revelation of the love of God. He knew that tribulation could not separate him from the love of God! I quote what he said from the Amplified Bible because it's so adamant:

'*For I am convinced [and continue to be convinced—beyond any doubt] that neither death, nor life, nor angels, nor principalities, nor things present and threatening, nor things to come, nor powers, nor height, nor depth, nor any other created thing, will be able to separate us from the [unlimited] love of God, which is in Christ Jesus our Lord.*' Romans 8:39

There is a wonderful picture in the Old Testament story of Ruth; Boaz the man who rescued her was her 'goel hadam.' The 'goel hadam' is a person who in the Old Testament culture is the nearest relative of another, the one who has the duty of restoring the rights of another and is charged with righting their wrongs. What a picture of what Jesus does for us!

God showed me that Jesus is my goel hadam.

When Ruth goes to the threshing floor at night, whilst Boaz is asleep, she covers herself with the edge of his garment. We used to sing a beautiful chorus in my early Christian days about Jesus, which makes me cry even as I write this:

'Cover me... cover me... extend the borders of your garments over me... because you are my nearest kinsman... cover me, cover me...cover me.'

I was so comforted by knowing that Jesus is my nearest kinsman, my *'goel hadam'* who will act on my behalf to bring justice!

Beyond doubt I know Jesus is mine, and all that He **has**, and all that He **is**, is mine.

It is vitally important to understand the truth that it is God's will to heal, but more than that, it is making it personal. It involves accepting that it is God's will to heal **ME**; because I've had it revealed to me by the Word of God and **owned it. I've made it mine!**

How wonderful that every promise that God has made is confirmed by the Holy Spirit who lives in me. The Holy Spirit acts as the guarantor of what we have.

'For all the promises of God in Him are Yes, and in Him Amen, to the glory of God through us. Now He who establishes us with you in Christ and has anointed us is God, who also has sealed us and given us the Spirit in our hearts as a guarantee.' 2 Corinthians 1:20-22

By the spirit that He has put in me, I can be like faithful Abraham, praising God for what He has promised, knowing that if He has promised something, He has the power to do it!

Abraham, we're told, '*did not waver concerning the promise of God but he grew strong empowered by faith, giving glory to God- fully convinced that he had the power to do what he had promised.*' Romans 4:20

Whatever interpretations can be made of any individual Scriptures, like Paul's thorn, Job's misfortunes, people who seem to have been left sick in the Acts of the Apostles, in my mind, all arguments are ended when we understand that the cross is **THE** pivotal point in the bible, and the turning-point in history.

How amazing that what Jesus did on the cross, He did for me! I can now rejoice that I have an unbreakable covenant which was made between Christ and God, made with the shed blood of Christ Himself, and simply because **I'm in Christ,** *by that very fact* I'm a partaker of it. It has become personal!

Because we believed in the power of the blood, Tony and I would take communion together to celebrate the effective power of the cross and our personal covenant with God. As we took the bread and the wine together, we would solemnly remember that on the cross Jesus broke that curse for me, He bore sin and sickness for me, so that I don't have to bear if. I am now a partaker of a great exchange: my sin was exchanged for His righteousness; my sickness was exchanged for His health.

God chose throughout the Bible to affirm His promises by blood covenant, to show that He really meant what he said. I would often plead the blood over my body, over my sickness, invoking the power of that blood by doing so.

What wonderful assurance we can have by knowing that by Christ's work on the cross, I am redeemed from the curse of the law, because he bore every curse.

"Christ has redeemed us from the curse of the law, having become a curse for us for it is written, "Cursed is everyone who hangs on a tree.' Galatians 3.13

The nature of curses and blessings are spelled out clearly in Deuteronomy 28. We could search in there for our sickness and be disappointed not to find it but verse 61 assures us that even if our sickness is not written there its included!

'Also, every sickness and every plague, <u>which is not</u> written in this Book of the Law, will the LORD *bring upon you until you are destroyed.'*

Therefore, I can put those two Scriptures; Deuteronomy 28.61 and Galatians 3.13 together and say this simple phrase:

According to Deuteronomy 28.61, **all sickness is a curse of the law so my sickness, cancer, is a curse of the law, but, according to Galatians 3:13 I am redeemed from the curse of the law by Christ Jesus who was made a curse for me. Therefore, I do not have cancer.**

It's good to say that phrase often to yourself. Say it out loud if you are alone, but under your breath if people are with you.

Our own personal belief about sickness is a key to receiving healing.

If Jesus called sickness 'oppression' and 'the work of the evil one', I must agree with Him. If you have any thoughts that God made you sick or wants you sick for some spiritual reason, your faith will waver.

Some people say that God has allowed a sickness to teach us things.

Of course, God may well teach us things during a time of sickness and may well bring good out of it, but that does not mean that he brought it or desired it. If sickness was God's will and intention, He would be working against Himself when, in fact, *'Jesus went about all Galilee, teaching in their synagogues, preaching the gospel of the kingdom, and healing all kinds of sickness and all kinds of disease among the people.'* Matthew 4:23

If Jesus delivered people from sickness when it was not the will of God for Him to do so, He would have been a very disobedient son indeed. I cannot say this more strongly: whatever you have been told, sickness is not the blessing of God; it's not the way He disciplines His children; it's not the way He accomplishes His will; it is not 'the means' He uses to teach us something.

Jesus Himself could only defeat sickness and destroy the works of the devil because **GOD was with him,** it says clearly.

'For <u>this purpose,</u> the Son of God was manifested, that He might <u>destroy the works of the devil.</u>' 1 John 3:8

That's the very reason He came to earth! Then we read yet again… *'How God anointed Jesus of Nazareth with the Holy Spirit and with power, who went about <u>healing all who were oppressed of the devil for God was with Him.</u>'* Acts 10:38

BUT stop waiting for your healing: its already in you!

I had prayer from many people, for which I was extremely grateful, including some faithful ones who came regularly. They were anointed and I was always blessed by their prayers. However, I was never simply waiting for God to heal me through other people; because I know that the Healer Himself and the power of God lives within me. I am a temple of the Holy Spirit: a vessel.

Yes, healing does come through people's hands and the words that they speak over us. The Bible says that *we will lay our hands on the sick and they will recover*, but actually HIS resurrection power is always at work in us, because He has made His home in us. *"My body is a temple of the Holy Spirit who is within me, which I have received as a gift from God and that I am not my own property... I was bought with a price... purchased with the precious blood of Jesus and made His very own."* 1 Corinthians 6:19.

Therefore, because of that, I **WILL** glorify God in my body. It's certain!

So, what is so great about the fact that He lives in me? Well, I can often feel His indwelling presence, and because of that, I know that He will give life to my physical body. *'But if the Spirit of Him who raised Jesus from the dead dwells in you, He who raised Christ from the dead will also give life to your mortal bodies through His Spirit who dwells in you.'* Romans 8:11.

It's the amazing power of His Spirit that works in us, doing exceedingly abundantly more that I could ask or think! If you think about it, that's awesome. It means that He is not limited by the smallness of our minds. We often cannot think big, especially when we don't feel well, and we make requests that are far too small, requests that are limited by our weak faith. When I felt so ill, my faith often felt very weak! BUT His promise is that He's not limited by our limited thinking and asking.

'Now to Him who is able to do exceedingly abundantly above all that we ask or think, according to the power that works in us, to Him be glory in the church by Christ Jesus to all generations, forever and ever.' Ephesians 3:21.

Healing cannot happen by our own effort; it happens by the power that works within us. However, we can activate our healing as we use our faith to cooperate with God

I really believe that it is His good pleasure to heal me. *'For it is God who works in you both to will and to do for His good pleasure.'* Philippians 2:13.

So: we need to expand our thinking. Think bigger. Don't think about our ability but think about HIS almighty ability. He is the God who created the universe.

Think about HIS treasure within us… it is the Spirit of God, the same spirit that raised Jesus Christ from the dead. It is the sweet and wonderful Holy Spirit that lives in us. It's very precious, because indeed it's HIS treasure. *'But we have this treasure in earthen vessels that the excellence of the power may be of God and not of us.'* 2 Corinthians 4:7.

Faith in His Word and the joy of His presence in worship, declaration and meditation stirred that power up in me, causing it to work mightily in me.

Many times, the words of songs ministered to me, stirring up that power. Years ago, there was one song by John Pantry that really spoke into my situation at that time and brought me faith and joy. I played this track over and over, often very loudly. When I was sick, I remembered this song. It says:

'If I should lose something of no value to me… I wouldn't mind if I couldn't find it again. But if it cost the earth, I would take great care not to lose it… but keep it always there.'

'Now we are not our own for we have been bought with a great price the blood of our dear Lord has been poured out for us and though the world may never understand we are in his hands and he will never lose what he holds so dear. Never fear…'

'He will take great care to hide us where the devil cannot look so rejoice my friend because your name is written in His book.'

I found that this song had the same power for me this time as it had before. I listened to it a lot! I knew God had paid a great price for me, I cost the earth to Him, and all this time that he was taking care of me and hiding me under His wings.

There was also a Don Moen song that I loved. He says:

"Let's believe God for our healing," and then sings the beautiful healing song: *"I am the God that healeth thee, I am the Lord your healer. I sent my word and healed your disease; I am the Lord your healer."*

Then he makes it personal to us and he changes it to; *"You are the Lord that healeth **me**; You are the Lord **my** healer. You sent your word and healed **my** disease; You are the Lord **my** healer."*

This song truly ministered to me, dozens and dozens of times!

I believe that the enemy cannot bear to hear us praising God because it destroys his work and wreaks judgement on him. It says according to Psalm 149:8-9; *'Let the high praises of God be in their mouth, and a two-edged sword in their hand, to execute vengeance on the nations, And punishments on the peoples; To bind their kings with chains, And their nobles with fetters of iron; To execute on them the written judgement— This honour have all His saints.'*

I could certainly sing aloud on my bed even when I didn't feel like it, if it executed judgement on my enemy and his sickness. It's about all I could do at times.

CHAPTER 11

How to secure what God has given you...

I was sure of my God given authority!

As believers, *God* has given <u>each of us</u> authority over sickness and over all the power of the enemy, which we must exercise to ensure that we receive what he wants us to have. '*For if by the one man's offence death reigned through the one, much more those who receive abundance of grace and of the gift of righteousness <u>will reign in life through the One, Jesus Christ.</u>' Romans 5:17*

We can receive the abundance of grace or ability, because we've already received the gift of righteousness - we are no longer just forgiven sinners, but we are the righteousness of God in Christ. Because of that, we can stand in the same authority that Jesus gave to his disciples in Mark 16. We reign as Kings in life, under the King of Kings.

I have authority over my circumstances as I walk with God listening to His wisdom and instructions. I don't have to live under my circumstances, because he has raised me up to sit with Him in the heavenly places above those circumstances.

We need to Believe that we have received it before we see it!

Another factor to successful receiving is believing that we have received our healing **before we see** the manifestation of it and not be afraid to **say** what God is doing.

I was bold enough to say: '***I shall not die, but live, and declare the works of the LORD.***' Psalm 118:17. I have heard some people describe this as living from the answer not from the problem; or living from heaven to earth, rather than living from earth to heaven. But faith receives the answer before it is seen. After all, we don't need faith, do we, after we see the answer? Jesus says two things, that we must believe that we have received before we see the answer, and then say so.

'*Now in the morning, as they passed by, they saw the fig tree dried up from the roots. And Peter, remembering, said to Him, "Rabbi, look! The fig tree which You cursed has withered away. So, Jesus answered and said to them, "Have faith in God. For assuredly, I say to you, whoever says to this mountain, 'Be removed and be cast into the sea,' and does not doubt in his heart, but believes that those things he says will be done, he will have whatever he says. Therefore, I say to you, whatever things you ask when you pray, believe that you receive them, and you will have them.'*
Mark 11:20-24

'Believe that you receive them and you will have them, Jesus says; '*and does not doubt in his heart but believes that those things HE SAYS will be done.*'

We further obey His instructions by saying it.

In this instance Jesus did not say that we would have what we **pray** but we would have what we ***say***. People sneer at what they call the *name it and claim it* brigade; BUT Jesus says clearly that we must ***say*** it, not just believe it in our heart.

I have always been struck by what it says in the parable in Luke 19 about the man whom the master calls '*the wicked servant.*' It shows me how much importance God places on what we say about Him and how the words of our mouths affect the way we behave. The servant says how he believes that the master is a harsh man, and then the master says something quite scary; *"I will judge you by using your own words."* I don't want my words to be used against me by my master. I want to be found in agreement with him; that He is good, that He is my healer!

Paul believed that speaking what he believed was important when he said; *'I believe therefore I speak.'* 2 Corinthians 4:13. So, I believed and spoke Scripture, and to help me receive them as directly for me, I wrote out all these the words and Scriptures into the first person, and I would declare them over myself every day. As I do that: I believe that; *'His word will not return to Him void but will accomplish that which he sent it for.'* (Isaiah 55:10.) God's Word will not return to Him void when we speak it out loud, boldly.

I obtained a book by Kynan Bridges called *'90 Days to Possessing Your Healing.'* In the book there is a section to meditate on, and then a prayer or confession to say. I meditated on the first section so that I understood it, internalised it so that I wasn't just saying it like a parrot, and then spoke out loud the second part. It was so faith-building!

I've seen in Scripture that everything miraculous happens from Creation onwards by speaking, through the power of words. God created everything by words. He spoke things into existence. The prophets spoke Jesus into existence throughout the Old Testament, saying who He was, and what He would do. Jesus spoke to sickness and disease and it left their bodies.

It should be no surprise that we can do the same because we are made in the image of a creative God who spoke the world into being. Our faith-filled words, just as His did, have the power to manifest the treasures of heaven. How thrilling that the angels will hear God's word when we speak it and move on our behalf.

'Bless the LORD, *you His angels, who excel in strength, who* **do His word**, *Heeding the voice of His word.'* Psalm 103:20. As we speak God's word, His angels will put it into action!

In Mark 11, it says that we are to **have the faith of God**; or you could say: a faith just **like** God's faith, which is exercised in God's way. In this passage of scripture, Jesus cursed the fig tree and it withered and died. Consequently, I believe that we can:

• Curse our sickness.
• Command our sickness to wither from the root.
• Speak to the sickness, (the mountain) and tell it to go!
• Believe what we say and receive it done without doubting in our heart.

People sent me many prayer confessions which I was able to use for myself. These consisted of scriptures personalised for me and put together in a way that I could say them effortlessly.

This is a confession a friend sent to me which I spoke out boldly and found very helpful: "*Lord, I declare that by the stripes of Jesus I am already healed because every sickness coming against me was nailed on the cross with you. Jesus, you took it upon yourself and so healing already belongs to me. In the name of Jesus, I bind the spirit of cancer and premature death and I break its power over my body. I curse the root of this disease – that it be dried up from the root and wither and die just like the fig tree withered and died when Jesus cursed it I declare that the blood supply is cut off from the mutated cells and they cannot prosper. I command my body to create killer cells to seek out and destroy every cancerous and mutant cell and when the job is done come down to normal levels. In Jesus name and by the power of the Spirit I speak a creative miracle of a brand-new immune system in my body after the treatment is finished. I command all of my cells to submit to God's will and God's word and function as God designed them to function. I plead the blood of Jesus over my cells to wash them of all ungodly influence and disease. I cleanse my brain from every stored hurt and pain and bring it all under God's control.*"

Another friend, called Dee, whom I met in California sent this; "*Lymphoma is a name and we have authority over every name with the name of Jesus which is more powerful than any other name I have authority to use the word of God – the blood of the lamb and the name of Jesus to defeat the enemy. Jesus died on the cross for all Margaret's sins and all Margaret's diseases. The word of God says that if two shall agree on earth concerning anything it will be done for them …In His name He will do it. So, in the name of Jesus we say to lymphoma. GO! Get off Margaret's body. She is covered with the blood of Jesus. I decree and declare that her lymph system is healthy and well and free from any symptoms of the enemy. I decree health and wholeness to every area of her body in Jesus name!*"

Proverbs 4:20 is clear. This is probably the third time I have quoted this scripture because it is so important... '*My son, give attention to my words; incline your ear to my sayings. Do not let them depart from your eyes; Keep them in the midst of your heart; for they are life to those who find them, and health to all their flesh. Keep your heart with all diligence, for out of it spring the issues of life. Put away from you a deceitful mouth and put perverse lips far from you.*'

To incline your ear… is vital. Have you seen the way an animal cocks its ear? And changes the direction of its ear to hear properly, fully alert, wanting to miss nothing? The clink of the lead or the dog dish, the word '*walkies*', is enough to make a dog do this. We must do this with HIS Word. We must read His Word, treasure His words, and incubate them in our hearts. The condition of our heart is so important because; '*Out of the abundance of the heart the mouth speaks.*' Matthew 12:34

Didn't Jesus say that we were defiled, not by what goes into our bodies, but by what comes out of our mouth! In other words, keep the Word in first place, give it your full attention, and don't speak negative things!

Sometimes I would read Scriptures together with Tony or my faithful supporter Claire. Did I feel like it? No, seldom… but that's when I needed it most! Did I sound full of faith? I don't think so but every time I read them out loud, I believe that they were a blow to the enemy's work in my body.

I also kept out of agreement with the negative reports of the medical profession. I didn't read the books that told me of the possible side effects. I found that Bill Johnson says: "*The enemy is empowered by human agreement. To agree with anything he says, gives him a place to kill steal and destroy. We fuel the cloud of oppression by agreement with our enemy. Praise with rejoicing cancels that agreement.*"

During a lot of the treatment when my brain seemed foggy and my body felt so weak, I found reading the Bible very difficult; but thankfully I could listen to it on my iPad or ask Alexa to open the Bible and read it to me. Then I could simply relax and listen to chapters over and over to milk them for revelation. I just let it wash over me, not trying to do anything with it, but just getting myself into a place where revelation could strike!

I kept my eyes on the Word of God, because sickness is a temporary condition, but the word of God is eternal, invisible but ever living. As Paul says; '*for we do not look at the things that are seen, but at the things that are not seen – for the things that are seen are temporary, but the things that are not seen are eternal.*' 2 Corinthians 4:18

Hebrews 4:2 says: '*the word of God is living and powerful, and sharper than any two-edged sword, piercing even to the division of soul and spirit.*' It's a spiritual weapon that God has given us with which to fight the fight of faith. It will pierce my being in the deepest places, where soul and spirit are, and do its work.

Faith in His word also brings joy in believing and great peace and confidence. So, we can have joy, just by believing in the process of healing, not only joy when we get the answer.

The Amplified version of Romans 15:13 says; *'May the God of hope fill you with all joy and peace in believing [through the experience of your faith] that by the power of the Holy Spirit you will abound in hope and overflow with confidence in His promises.'*

The very fact that we are believing and not doubting brings hope and confidence.

CHAPTER 12

How I overcame fear

Earlier I said that apart from two occasions during the treatment, I'd had great peace in my heart. I will now tell you about those two occasions when that peace left.

The first occasion when I felt fear, if not sheer terror, was when I received a letter from the consultant saying that they could not promise that the treatment would work in a 73-year-old woman, nor that the sickness would not return. They said that there was a 50% chance of it returning. Mind you, that means there is also a 50% chance that it won't return!

Although I knew that this was the truth as far as the medical profession was concerned and that I was relying on a higher truth to deliver me, as I read this sentence it pierced my heart and I was utterly gripped with fear. It took me two days of paying attention to the Word of God, and going over His promises to me, before my peace returned.

The second time I lost my peace was just after the end of the treatment when I had been for the final scan. I woke up in the middle of the night feeling complete panic because of a fearful dream...

In the dream I was on the deck of a cruise ship. As I looked over the edge, I could see lots of people having fun in kayaks. They were waving and smiling and beckoning me to join them, so I decided to climb down the big ladder on the side of the ship. I had a lovely time with them and then decided it was time to get back onto the ship.

It was a long way up as it was a huge ship. As I climbed, I felt more and more tired, and just before I got to the top I suddenly panicked because I felt that I did not have the strength to get back onto the boat. Terrified, I clung to the ladder absolutely paralysed. I felt that any minute my grip would fail, and I would fall down into the water. Then I woke up!

As I lay there shaking with fear, I had awful words going through my head… '*What if God doesn't exist at all…what if I'm totally deceived… what if I'm not healed and after all these brave words I die!*'

Suddenly, I recognised the source of all these thoughts…the enemy… I knew satan would not give up his plan to finish my life easily, so I shook Tony awake and told him about it. Sleepily he said: "*SING!*" "*Sing?*" I said; "*I don't want to sing!*"

He began sleepily singing an old chorus that we both knew, which is full of God's Word, and I knew that I literally had to force myself to join in. That did it! Once I began to sing too, the fear broke! For about half an hour we sang all the old choruses that we could think of and ended up laughing and rejoicing together. I was not troubled again by that fear and slept peacefully for the rest of the night.

How funny that there a Psalm that encourages us to do this; '*Let the saints be joyful in glory, let them sing aloud on their beds.*' Psalm 149:5 God's enemy, satan, who was attempting to make me afraid, was defeated that night!

When I prayed about it the next day, I felt God say that I had picked up a spirit of fear when I went to the hospital for that final scan. I can only imagine how many people feel very frightened in that place. I felt that this horrible dream coming just before that final scan showed that maybe a bit of me was afraid that I wasn't really healed. The next day I journalled:

Lord, I know that part of me is afraid that the scan will show that the cancer is still there. I feel so ashamed. Everyone thinks I am so positive, brave and full of faith and here I am feeling like this. This great woman of faith is full of fear today! Help me Lord to get back into faith and trust.

Jesus replied: *'What will you do about it if they say that the disease is still there? You will not change it by fretting or being upset about it. Focus on my promises as I have shown you. Worry will not change it but faith will. Do you really think I have led you this far to let you down? You know me better than that. Get into praise, get your attention off it and make your day joyful because I am in it with you.' 'Let the fear go my child. If it were true you could do nothing about it by keeping that fear alive. Let it go and let my peace reign. Believing that all things are possible with me and all things are possible to you because you believe. Do not spend the rest of this time nursing a fear that is a lie of the devil sent to take away your confidence in me. Keep your mind on what I have promised you and even what the consultant said who does not even know me. Stamp on that fear; be firm with it, stand up to the evil one: he is a liar and a thief.'*

Before I went for the appointment with the consultant I spoke out; *"I will not be afraid of evil tidings; my heart is fixed, trusting in the Lord. My heart is established. I will not be afraid until I see my desire upon my enemies." Psalm 112.7*

I was waiting in the room at the clinic for a little while, until two smiling nurses, and the consultant entered the room. He was grinning from ear to ear. Throwing his hands up triumphantly, he cried; *"Well, your scan was fantastic and you are in complete remission!"* Such good news; but I'm glad to say... it was only what I expected!

Now I have been given all clear: 'complete remission'. I know that now is not the time to slacken my grip on the Word of God; but of course, I'm not expecting evil tidings! 'I will also believe and say, Nahum 1:9; *'What do you conspire against the* LORD*? He will make an utter end of it. Affliction will not rise up a second time.'*

Also Psalm 91:16; 'With *long life I will satisfy him and show him My salvation.'*
And Psalm 118:17; 'I *shall not die, but live, and declare the works of the* LORD*.'*

I am sure that*: 'For I know the plans I have for you – plans for your welfare not for disaster –to give you a future and a hope.'* Jeremiah 29:11

I think it has to be miraculous that within one month after the final treatment I felt well and strong and back to completely normal life; enjoying cooking, cleaning, shopping, trips out to social events, etc. I simply woke up one morning and felt like a new woman: my normal self! I got out of bed and cooked Tony's egg and mushroom breakfast, probably the first time in five months. He was very surprised and delighted to see it!

The first thing I enjoyed doing in the kitchen was to make marmalade and blackberry jelly. I'd had those blackberries in the freezer since the previous autumn but until then I'd felt too ill to do anything with them.

The second thing was to make bread and enjoy eating it. Vacuuming and washing the floor became a joy, not a chore. Oh, how good it was to have the strength to do ordinary things!

When I spoke to the Lord in this time, I said: "*Lord I'm so glad to be alive and healed and full of joy. I'm thankful for all those who have stood with me, being strong for me when I felt so weak. I am so blessed.*"

He said: "*Indeed you are blessed ...blessed is she who believed what God had told her. They said about my mother, and you are as precious to me as my mother: you have the favour of heaven upon your life… Enjoy the fruits of it. Seeking first my kingdom and my righteousness has brought great reward to you. Knowing me and knowing my Word has delivered you. If all my children were the same it would give me such joy and make my sacrifice a greater joy. keep your heart pure… keep your mind clear and continue to keep your focus on me ...there is much to come.*"

One chemo nurse had told me that it would take me as long to recover as it took me to have the treatment. "*Five months?*" I said. "*Oh no it won't!*" At my appointment, two weeks after the final scan, the consultant told me that it would be at least two months before I even started to feel well. "*Just remember,*" he said, "*you have had six strong sessions of chemotherapy and you were very, **very** sick.*"

Thankfully, God's schedule is obviously different from theirs! I told him: "I'm sorry but it's too late to tell me that, I already feel completely well."

In parts of Psalm 116, I found my whole story; '*I love the* LORD, *because He has heard my voice and my supplications because He has inclined His ear to me, Therefore I will call upon Him as long as I live. The pains of death surrounded me, and the pangs of Sheol laid hold of me; I found trouble and sorrow. Then I called upon the name of the* LORD: "*O* LORD, *I implore You, deliver my soul! For You have delivered my soul from death, my eyes from tears and my feet from falling. I will walk before the* LORD *in the land of the living. What shall I render to the* LORD *For all His benefits toward me? I will take up the cup of salvation and call upon the name of the* LORD. *I will pay my vows to the* LORD, *now in the presence of all His people.*'

So that's what I'm doing right now!

People constantly say how well I look and recently when I went for a check-up in October 2019, just eighteen months after I was declared free of lymphoma, the consultant said; "*You look so well; you look much younger than 75!*" After a two-year check-up, the consultant said. "*If it has not returned for two years, it's unlikely to return*" It was wonderful to hear that. My wellness is such a great tool for witnessing to the goodness of God.

One day during this time when I had journaled, God said: "*I told you to do like Jesus did. Take authority over the storm - get to the other side and shine! This has been an ideal opportunity for you to demonstrate who you are. and who I am. It has made a platform for you to stand on. It will be such a blessing to others!*"

I said: "but Lord, I was not ready for this attack!" He said to me; "*You were not ready but I was – I knew that it was coming and I prepared you well in advance for it. You had an arsenal of weapons and most of all the ability to hear me and follow my instructions. The fruit of years of diligence and preparation swung into action and the world and the church have seen the stunning result. Your total health and healing are far more than any medical help could produce by itself. It is far above and beyond. Well done my child for demonstrating my overcoming ability and the amazing strength that resides in you. WE are victorious …you and I together!*"

CHAPTER 13

Will the disease come back?

This is the question that many ask.

We do hear of many instances that cancer comes back; and I believe that it's a fear, or even dread, that many people wrestle with. Indeed, I had far more moments of fear after the treatment than I ever had during it! That's why, when you get the all-clear, it's not the time to take faith pressure off. It is time to take a stronger stand than ever. Put your spiritual foot down and refuse the sickness access to your life.

What should you do?

Well, the **worst** thing you could do is to live in fear of its return, especially if the prognosis from the medical world is not good. Although I took a strong stand, I found that any symptom in my body had the power to raise an alarm in my heart… "Is this the cancer coming back?"

During one hospital visit, I was also made to fear that I would have another thrombosis. When I saw the consultant, he had said in a seemingly unnecessarily strong and definite way; *"You WILL have another one."* That remark was spoken with such ferocity and faith that for some time it really troubled me.

So, after this, one day I had a pain and what felt like a lump behind my knee, and so I asked to get checked out at the hospital. I was given a scan, a blood test and two examinations by two different doctors who both told me to go home because I was as fit as a fiddle! And yet, still this fear kept rising, resulting in a further examination on another day.

That second time that I gave way to this fear, I was so angry and disgusted with myself for allowing it *heart-room* that I put my foot down and said with determination; "Devil, that's enough! You are a liar and I'm not having this anymore! I command the fear of thrombosis to leave and never come back!" Then every time after that when I felt the least bit nervous about it I'd say; "*Oh no you don't, that's enough, my blood does not clot when it shouldn't and it flows easily though my veins!*"

I sometimes feel that it's easier being diagnosed with cancer, than it is living after the event. I talked to a Macmillan nurse one day and she said: "*It's because, once you've had it, you have to live with it.*" Health professionals are well aware of this problem, and they are understanding and easy to talk to about it. If you can't get to one, talk to a good friend and ask them to pray with you. Don't give in to it, but on the other hand, don't ignore anything that is alarming enough to be the real thing!

I've relied on the strength of my faith in God and His word, but fortunately the medical team have immediately pounced on anything that looked suspicious. I only had to flag up a difficulty and they'd re-examine me, and once when the pain was very like the one I'd had at the beginning, they offered me an extra scan, which of course came back perfectly clear.

Twice in the last year I've had suspicious pains, once in my upper abdomen just like the ones I had when I was very sick, and another, a lump in my breast which was investigated and proved to be nothing.

For a while I had to keep fighting to keep that awful fear from coming back and I often felt tense and nervous as check-up's drew near. In every instance I would return to the things God had said to me in the midst of the battle and the particular Scriptures that were such a comfort to me, and I would also bring to mind the prophecies I'd had about the future.

One day, when I was telling Tony how I felt, he looked me in the eye and said: "Nahum 1:9; '*This affliction shall not come a second time.*'" Immediately peace entered my heart.

Many cancer survivors will tell you the same thing: that with every pain or ache there is a temptation to believe that the cancer has come back or that cancer has come in yet a new place. Of course, some people are told that the cancer is likely to return, in which case the fear is fuelled by those statements, or maybe they are told that the cancer cannot be treated.

It can be a lie.

I encourage you to <u>make it a lie</u> by fighting it with God's truth!

I think as Christians we need something of the spirit of Churchill when he said…

"We will fight them on the beaches, we will fight them on the landing grounds, we shall fight them in the field… We shall fight them in the hills… WE SHALL NEVER SURRENDER!"

From the start I knew that this whole situation was a faith battle and that my faith must stand firm. The Word must still be '*kept in the midst of my heart*'; because God calls the Word His medicine.

Any pain can start the fear. When we were on holiday in Greece, I began to be plagued with pains in my stomach! I sat beside the pool with my journalling book, and wrote: *'Lord, today I'm plagued again with fear - it's low level yes, but I'm in fear about the return of the cancer. I have pains in my stomach and I'm feeling more tired than usual.'*

He said: *"Settle your heart, my dear one, that I have a future and a hope for you, and that this affliction will not come a second time. I healed you, it was not just chemotherapy that made you well. I am your God and I am El Shaddai. I can do far above all that you can ask or think. Tell those fears to go and not return, then enjoy your holiday with relaxation and sunshine."*

I said: *"I can see you, Lord, sitting on the end of the sunbed here... just as you promised you would be, but I now also sense your comfort and your presence in me"*

I heard Him saying; *"I want you to sense my anointing, my presence, completely filling your whole body, giving you rest and peace. See me in every lymph node... blessing them...see me in your vital organs... see me dissolving gall stones and kidneys stones. I am your healer. I am ever present in your body working. When you were afraid it was because your heart and mind were elsewhere fixed on your difficulties, and it became very costly for you. Do not ever go down that road again... stay with your heart fixed on me... whatever happens!"*

After that I relaxed, the pain went, and I enjoyed my holiday!

People often encouraged me to get every pain I felt checked out, but I said; *"Look, if I allow myself to be pushed by this fear, I'm giving place to the enemy. If I fall for it this time, he will only try all the harder to get my attention!"*

However, I'm glad to report a complete end to this anxiety. It happened one day when I went to a ladies' meeting where the speaker was talking about anxiety. At the end of her talk she said: *"Take your anxiety, whatever it's about, and give it to the Lord."*

Right then, as I focused on Jesus, I had a strange vison. I saw myself holding an envelope in my hand, and I knew that it contained all my fear and anxiety about the return of cancer. Jesus was standing in front of me, and He had a strange opening in His belly just like a post box. I saw myself posting that package of anxiety into that 'post box', just as if it were a letter or parcel. Immediately I had let it go, I had an amazing sense of finality.

"*There,*" I said, as I turned to my friend, "*I know that I'll never experience that anxiety again!*" She looked at me blankly because she hadn't a clue what I was talking about, but for me it was a moment of faith! Since then I have never felt that fear again. After that 'special moment' I went for my yearly review, and the letter that followed restated my disease status. It said: '*There was an excellent response to the treatment after 2 cycles and her full blood count is normal, there is no palpable lymphadenopathy and no organomegaly, complete remission.*' I'm so glad that the reassurance came after I'd let the anxiety go!

Jesus said to me...*"The walk of faith always pleases me. The just, the righteous are to live by faith in me, and moreover, to enjoy living with faith in me. I know that we both enjoy it. It is the secret life that has the open reward."*

Remember, we don't live looking for the devil; but we do need to remember that his job description is to steal, kill and destroy. He'd like to steal your peace He'd like to steal everything a believer has in Christ. So, be alert and make sure he can't steal from you! It's him who would like to torment you about every pain and tell you it's your cancer returned. Use your God-given authority to send him packing!

CHAPTER 14

It's time to celebrate and shout!

Many times, throughout the Bible, we read God telling His people to "Shout!", for He had given them the victory. What the devil wants is for you and me to be held hostage with the fear of a disease. One way to break fear is the victory shout! Yes, that is right, even if you have to drive out to the countryside and let the roar, roar until you feel the fear snapping inside. When that happens, a new life will shine through you.

Briefly, and lastly, as we are rejoicing and shouting the victory, there are twenty things I'd like to remind you to do!

Cultivate gratitude and thanksgiving.

Make worship a daily part of your life.

Keep your heart steady.

If, like me, you experienced events and pains which were part of your journey to sickness, don't just live with it. Always take it to the Lord. Learn how to dialogue with Him. Write out your *'prayers'* and tell Him what you are feeling and thinking. It doesn't matter whether what you think is 'right or wrong', or whether you think is good or bad! Be honest with Him. It's just between you and Him. Then listen to what He wants to say about it. As you listen to the flowing thoughts that come into your mind, write them down so that you record His heavenly perspective on the matter. This is one of the major ways I keep my heart steady.

Let Him speak peace and healing into your heart. by learning how to dialogue with God. This is such an important thing to do as it will develop your intimacy and friendship with God in a wonderful way. It's as simple as learning Four Keys, which we call journalling:

1. **Quieten yourself down**… find a quiet place… play some wordless worship music or speak the Word quietly and meditatively to yourself.

2. **Fix your eyes on Jesus**… get a picture of where Jesus is with you, in your mind's eye, which offers him the chance to create a true vision.

3. **Tune-in to spontaneity**… in other words, simply catch those flowing thoughts that are popping into your head.

4. **Write them down**…. record what you think you are hearing.

You could go onto our website; www.HearingGodsVoiceUK.net and get a copy of '*4 keys to hearing God's Voice*,' which will explain it all thoroughly.

There is also some wonderful journalling music to use as you journal, on Mark Virkler's website. You can download it free: it's called, '*A Stroll Along the Sea of Galilee.*'

You could also look on our website to see if there is a 'Four Keys' seminar being held in a church near you. Or you could invite our team to *your* church to do a seminar. Here's another sample of my own journalling to encourage you to do this:

"Margaret… you have grasped the principal thing, which is to live your life depending on Me and looking to Me for your needs to be met for healing, strength and all that I can supply. You went to Bethel to receive more anointing and a greater impartation of my grace and glory, to minister to others and heal the sick.

"How could I refuse to give you this wonderful gift, and to lift your heart and mind into a place of greater expectation. You will experience my healing and also my gifting. Thank you, dear child, for sharing my love for people and my desire to see them healed. Through it I can draw people to myself. Healing is one of the ways I can do this. It is my greatest pleasure to see wholeness in my children, spirit, soul and body. I want my children to be advertisements of my glory and advertisements of my ability to meet their needs. The world must be made jealous by my body. That was my intention with Israel and is my continued intention with you, my covenant people. You see…I never change!"

On another occasion I said to Him: "Jesus, *for the first time I really noticed that you called God your Father and my Father… When you had risen from the tomb you said; "Do not cling to Me, for I have not yet ascended to My Father; but go to My brethren and say to them, 'I am ascending to* **My Father and your Father**, *and to* **My God and your God**.*'" Of course, I knew that He was our Father; but it impacted me afresh today as I read the Scripture."*

Jesus said to me: *"Can you see the privilege that we both have? We are both linked to the Father –linked to a father, not just a god. Many religions have a god but none have a Father as we have. You and I are His children because He gave birth to both of us. He gave birth to Me before the foundation of the world and He gave birth to you when you met Me and you were born of His Spirit. Because you are born of Him you can't help being like Him. Just as you see in your DNA in the natural the similarities that you have with your natural parents, you are like Him. Enjoy being made in His image - all made possible because of the work of the Holy Spirit. Dear Holy Spirit, how I love Him and how I know that He does all things well! He will promote you as you develop more relationship with Him …just as He did with me."*

Wow! I love it when He speaks to me and shares His heart with me like this; and so will you!

The purity of your heart is very precious to the Lord, so guard your heart… Never **stay** angry and upset, allow Him to process hurts and events with you.

Make up your mind to forgive, freely, quickly, decisively and thoroughly,

Don't wait until you feel like doing it. Forgiveness is a decision, not a feeling.

Learn how to apologise appropriately when you realise something was your fault. Don't just say *I'm sorry*, it's much more effective to say, *will you forgive me*? Jesus came to earth to bring reconciliation with the Father and also reconciliation between people We always called it *keeping short accounts*. The Word tells us, that we should strive to be at peace with others.

Get rid of bitterness, criticism, resentment, fear, lust; in fact anything negative and sinful. These negative emotions and ways of behaving are so exhausting. Held long-term are likely to make you sick.

Maybe you feel that you need a deeper level of help to be able to do this, and if you do… get counselling. There are many therapies that the health service offer. Take advantage of them.

Find some good friends, join a cancer support group, or some kind of social group, and try being a good friend to others. Be brave and seek to support those who are now in the position that you were in.

Live your life with an outward focus.

Think…. how can I make someone else feel loved, and be their friend? Maybe you could sometimes send them a little encouraging note or buy something small that you know that they will like; telephone them; send a loving text; pray for them! I've been inspired lately by the idea of doing random acts of kindness or just simply telling someone, even a stranger, how nice they look, or just tell someone something about them that you admire. Doing this has often given me enormous joy. Just to see their reaction is such fun. Get the focus of your life off yourself!

Remember you authority in Christ …its yours.

Learn to have fun and laugh.

Laughter is such a good medicine! Laughter can increase essential blood flow, laughter can reduce pain, Laughter can prevent disease, laughter can improve emotional health. Laughter can strengthen your spirit. Resist the devil with JOY!

I don't have much trust for the truth of the media, so I don't watch the television news unless there's something specific that I feel I need to watch a small amount of. I gave up reading newspapers for the same reason. I know how I've been lied about in newspaper reports, and they cannot always be trusted. I'm also very careful what kinds of films or programmes I watch on the television. In general, most of it is ungodly and destructive.

As much as you can, keep negative people out of your life.,

If you live with them that's not so easy; but if you can at least ration the amount of access they have into your heart and your life.

Find a good church, if you don't have one.

This would be a church where they really believe and live the Bible by demonstrating the love of God.

Remind yourself daily of the healing Scriptures

Keep thanking the Lord for your healing and that His Word remains true whatever comes. As already mentioned, Dodi Osteen, whom I met in Houston in 1982, was diagnosed with metastatic cancer of the liver in 1981. Six months after her diagnosis she was still in the battle, and she still looked quite weak. She told us that she never lets a day go by without confessing healing scriptures. At 10.10am she cries; '*Oh no you don't, devil! Because in John 10:10, Jesus says; "The thief does not come except to steal, and to kill, and to destroy. I have come that they may have life, and that they may have it more abundantly." He's come to bring me abundant life!*'

When I saw her recently, nearly 30 years later, although she is in her 80's she looked so beautiful and radiant, and so well. I think that speaks for itself!

Eat well

I also believe that you can help yourself by seeing that you are not eating an unhealthy diet full of refined sugar, fried foods and processed food Definitely cut your sugar intake.

Take exercise

Take some exercise! It is so good for your strength and lifting your mood. It definitely helps people with depression, and it can help us build muscle and to lose a little weight healthily. Even 15 minutes a day they say makes a great deal of difference.

I used to hate walking; I think it was because I was forced to go for long walks with my parents as a child. But I have learned to love it!

Suddenly I realised how inactive I'd become. One day I had a blood test which showed that my triglycerides were high which is not a healthy thing. I googled how to lower them, and it suggested walking 150 minutes a week. I have now bought a Fitbit and try to walk as many steps as I can in a day. Today I only did 4,932 by 5.30pm which is 2.08 miles but I started with much less than that and I am hoping to move up to 10,000 some days. I've only done that one day so far in the months that I have been doing it, because that would probably take me an hour. Every day varies. Some days I have a friend with whom I walk, and other days I go on my own. I try to vary my routes around the village and I've not pushed myself, but just gradually increased what I can do. Instead of feeling tired by my walks, I now feel energised by them. They are great prayer times too.

If going out is not an option, then, like I did, get an exercise bike or small exercise machine. It's important to move our bodies! Try Pilates, Zumba, or whatever you can do to get the blood going around your body! Locally we have chair Pilates for people who cannot do the rather energetic exercises. Simple stretching every morning as you get out of bed will help. If you cannot manage very much… just do as much as you can.

Supplements

Maybe you could supplement your diet with at least vitamin D. Even the government is saying to watch out you are not short of vitamin D. You can see online where you can pay a small amount to get your vitamin D levels tested if your medical practitioner will not do it. Get into the sunshine, even 30 minutes a day boosts your vitamin D. I believe that supplementing my diet is a good idea, but not with cheap shop-bought products but with good quality vitamins and minerals, although this is a controversial subject and opinion is much divided on it.

I take curcumin, krill oil, vitamin D, vitamin B complex and Resveratrol. I have read good medical research that curcumin or turmeric deals with inflammation and is something that could keep lymphoma at bay. Take some good probiotics, but even a little live yogurt every day will help to keep your gut healthy.

There are many diets out there; but I believe that the *'Rainbow Diet,'* which is basically the Mediterranean diet, is the best to follow. This is a diet with lots of colourful fruit and vegetables, preferably as much organic as you can afford, with small amounts of chicken and fish and not so much red meat. You can buy a book of that name which has lots of technical information about assisting yourself with diet, and an accompanying recipe book, all of which are very helpful.

Vegetable smoothies, with a spoonful of green stuff added, like spirulina, and a minimal amount of fruit to add sweetness is a quick way of increasing nutrition and decreasing refined sugar intake. Home-made vegetable juices are also healthy additions to a good diet. Many years ago, I invested in a Samson masticating juicer, but a cheaper centrifugal one is a good second best. Better than nothing! You can get good diet and supplement advice from many sources, but you do need to maximise your nutrition. The website Canceractive is most helpful about all of this.

Keep things moving on

Eliminating the negative is not just about toxic emotion! Try to make sure you have a bowel motion every day. If your diet is okay and you have some exercise, that will ensure that, but if not, talk to your doctor or a reputable chemist, about what they recommend.

Watch your stress levels

You need to watch your stress levels. Learn how to say no to doing those things which you only do because you feel guilty. Let God guide you to do what is essential for you. Take moments out of your day to rest and play. Take up a hobby. Do things that you enjoy. Balance your life with work, rest and play. Try to programme things into your life that are fun!

Get 8 hours good sleep.

When we sleep, our body repairs itself. If you have poor sleep take, maybe you are short of Melatonin which is created by your pineal gland as you fall asleep.   We can't get Melatonin except on prescription in this country, but you can purchase something that will create Melatonin in your body. Always sleep in a darkened room.

Learn to give love and approval liberally to your family and friends.

When I was a little girl, several times I read 'The Water Babies' by Charles Kingsley. I'll never forget the characters '*Do as you would be done by*' and '*Be done by as you did*' Even as child I saw that those names contained wisdom. Things have a way of coming back on you later in life. Of course, the Bible tells us; *Do not be deceived, God is not mocked; for **whatever a man sows**, that he will also reap.* Galatians 6:7

Learn to live thankful for all you have.

A healthy, wholesome lifestyle makes you happy, and is good for your spirit, soul and body. However bad things are there is always something to be thankful for. It is the best defence against sickness!

Finally, I trust that you have been blessed by what you have read and I pray this for you:

Father God, help my readers to see that they are spiritual beings, created in your image, and deeply loved by you.

Give them a supernatural vision of the joy a pure heart and of a lifestyle spent in your presence.

Open their heart with spiritual revelation to see the truth of your Word.

Open their spiritual eyes to see the reality of the heavenly realm.

Teach them to speak words of faith that will transform them and the world that they see around them, into a representation of your heavenly kingdom on earth.

I pray that your will is done, and your kingdom comes in their body, soul and spirit.

Amen.

Why not think deeply about that and pray it for yourself putting it in the first person for example, Father God give **me, or** open **my...** etc.

Enjoy Margaret's Autobiography...

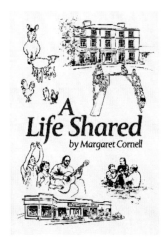

"A Life Shared" is set in a small village in Cambridgeshire, where in 1970 Margaret experienced a dramatic conversion, which led to her home being open to 65 people in 45 years. Alongside her husband, they led a thriving charismatic church in Ely for 25 years.

This Is an inspiring book, full of amazing answers to prayer and a lifestyle of loving and giving, which continues in their lives until today.

CONTACT THE AUTHOR
VISIT
www.HearingGodsVoiceUK.net

Inspired to write a book?

Contact

Maurice Wylie Media
Inspirational Christian Publisher

Based in Northern Ireland and distributing around the world.

www.MauriceWylieMedia.com

Scriptures that you will find in this book

1 Corinthians 6:19-20 *'Or do you not know that your body is the temple of the Holy Spirit who is in you, whom you have from God, and you are not your own? For you were bought at a price; therefore, glorify God in your body and in your spirit, which are God's.'*

1 John 3:8 *'For this purpose, the Son of God was manifested that He might destroy the works of the devil.'*

1 John 5:4 *'For whatever is born of God overcomes the world; and this is the victory that has overcome the world - our faith.'*

1 Peter 2:24 *'Who Himself bore our sins in His own body on the tree, that we, having died to sins, might live for righteousness—by whose stripes you were healed.'*

1 Peter 5:10 *'But may the God of all grace, who called us to His eternal glory by Christ Jesus, after you have suffered a while, perfect, establish, strengthen, and settle you.'*

1 Peter 5:8 *'Be sober, be vigilant; because your adversary the devil walks about like a roaring lion, seeking whom he may devour.'*

2 Corinthians 4:16-18 *'Therefore we do not lose heart. Even though our outward man is perishing, yet the inward man is being renewed day by day. For our light affliction, which is but for a moment, is working for us a far more exceeding and eternal weight of glory, while we do not look at the things which are seen, but at the things which are not seen. For the things which are seen are temporary, but the things which are not seen are eternal.'*

2 Corinthians 1:20 *'All the promises of God in Him are Yes, and in Him Amen, to the glory of God through us.'*

2 Corinthians 10:3 *'For though we walk in the flesh, we do not war according to the flesh.'*

2 Corinthians 4:7 *'But we have this treasure in earthen vessels, that the excellence of the power may be of God and not of us.'*

2 Corinthians 4:16-18 *'Therefore we do not lose heart. Even though our outward man is perishing, yet the inward man is being renewed day by day. For our light affliction, which is but for a moment, is working for us a far more exceeding and eternal weight of glory, while we do not look at the things which are seen, but at the things which are not seen. For the things which are seen are temporary, but the things which are not seen are eternal.'*

2 Kings 13:14-18 *'Elisha had become sick with the illness of which he would die. Then Joash the king of Israel came down to him, and wept over his face, and said, "O my father, my father, the chariots of Israel and their horsemen!" And Elisha said to him, "Take a bow and some arrows." So, he took himself a bow and some arrows. Then he said to the king of Israel, "Put your hand on the bow." So, he put his hand on it, and Elisha put his hands on the king's hands. And he said, "Open the east window"; and he opened it. Then Elisha said, "Shoot"; and he shot. And he said, "The arrow of the LORD's deliverance and the arrow of deliverance from Syria; for you must strike the Syrians at Aphek till you have destroyed them." Then he said, "Take the arrows"; so, he took them. And he said to the king of Israel, "Strike the ground"; so, he struck three times, and stopped. And the man of God was angry with him, and said, "You should have struck five or six times; then you would have struck Syria till you had destroyed it! But now you will strike Syria only three times."*

2 Kings 20:5 *"Return and tell Hezekiah the leader of My people, 'Thus says the LORD, the God of David your father: "I have heard your prayer, I have seen your tears; surely I will heal you. On the third day you shall go up to the house of the LORD.'*

2 Timothy 1:6 *'Therefore I remind you to stir up the gift of God which is in you through the laying on of my hands. For God has not given us a spirit of fear, but of power and of love and of a sound mind.'*

3 John 2 *'Beloved, I pray that you may prosper in all things and be in health, just as your soul prospers.'*

Acts 10:38 *'How God anointed Jesus of Nazareth with the Holy Spirit and with power, who went about doing good and healing all who were oppressed by the devil, for God was with Him.'*

Colossians 1:13 *'He has delivered us from the power of darkness and conveyed us into the kingdom of the Son of His love.'*

Deuteronomy 28:6 *'Blessed shall you be when you come in and blessed shall you be when you go out.'*

Deuteronomy 28:61 *'Also every sickness and every plague, which is not written in this Book of the Law, will the LORD bring upon you until you are destroyed.'*

Deuteronomy 33:27 *'The eternal God is your refuge, and underneath are the everlasting arms; He will thrust out the enemy from before you, and will say, 'Destroy!'*

Ephesians 3:14-18 *'For this reason I bow my knees to the Father of our Lord Jesus Christ, from whom the whole family in heaven and earth is named, that He would grant you, according to the riches of His glory, to be strengthened with might through His Spirit in the inner man, that Christ may dwell in your hearts through faith; that you, being rooted and grounded in love, may be able to comprehend with all the saints what is the width and length and depth and height—to know the love of Christ which passes knowledge; that you may be filled with all the fulness of God.'*

Ephesians 3:20 *'Now to Him who is able to do exceedingly abundantly above all that we ask or think, according to the power that works in us.'*

Ephesians 6:11 *'Put on the whole armour of God, that you may be able to stand against the wiles of the devil.'*

Exodus 15:26 *'And said, "If you diligently heed the voice of the LORD your God and do what is right in His sight, give ear to His commandments and keep all His statutes, I will put none of the diseases on you which I have brought on the Egyptians. For I am the LORD who heals you."*

Exodus 23:25 *"So you shall serve the LORD your God, and He will bless your bread and your water. And I will take sickness away from the midst of you.'*

Galatians 3:13 *'Christ has redeemed us from the curse of the law, having become a curse for us for it is written, "Cursed is everyone who hangs on a tree."*

Hebrews 10:23 *'Let us hold fast the confession of our hope without wavering, for He who promised is faithful.'*

Hebrews 11.6 *'But without faith it is impossible to please Him, for he who comes to God must believe that He is, and that He is a rewarder of those who diligently seek Him.'*

Hebrews 12:1 *'Therefore we also, since we are surrounded by so great a cloud of witnesses, let us lay aside every weight, and the sin which so easily ensnares us, and let us run with endurance the race that is set before us.'*
Hebrews 13:8 *'Jesus Christ is the same yesterday, today, and forever.'*

Isaiah 58 6:8 *"Is this not the fast that I have chosen: To loose the bonds of wickedness, to undo the heavy burdens, to let the oppressed go free, and that you break every yoke? Is it not to share your bread with the hungry,* *and that you bring to your house the poor who are cast out? When you see the naked, that you cover him, and not hide yourself from your own flesh? Then your light shall break forth like the morning, your healing shall spring forth speedily, and your righteousness shall go before you; and the glory of the LORD shall be your rear-guard.'*

Isaiah 41:13 *'For I, the LORD your God, will hold your right hand, saying to you, 'Fear not, I will help you.'*

Isaiah 43:2 *'When you pass through the waters, I will be with you; and through the rivers, they shall not overflow you. When you walk through the fire, you shall not be burned, nor shall the flame scorch you.'*

Isaiah 54:17 *'No weapon formed against you shall prosper, and every tongue which rises against you in judgment you shall condemn. This is the heritage of the servants of the LORD, and their righteousness is from Me," Says the LORD.'*

Isaiah 55:3-5 *'He is despised and rejected by men, a man of sorrows and acquainted with grief. And we hid, as it were, our faces from Him; He was despised, and we did not esteem Him. Surely He has borne our griefs And carried our sorrows; yet we esteemed Him stricken, smitten by God, and afflicted. But He was wounded for our transgressions, He was bruised for our iniquities. The chastisement for our peace was upon Him; and by His stripes we are healed.'*

Isaiah 53:10 *'Yet it pleased the LORD to bruise Him; He has put Him to grief. When You make His soul an offering for sin, He shall see His seed, He shall prolong His days, And the pleasure of the LORD shall prosper in His hand.'*

Isaiah 59:19 *'So shall they fear the name of the LORD from the west, and His glory from the rising of the sun; when the enemy comes in like a flood, the Spirit of the LORD will lift up a standard against him.'*

Isaiah 61:1-2 *'The Spirit of the Lord GOD is upon Me, because the LORD has anointed Me to preach good tidings to the poor; He has sent Me to heal the broken-hearted, to proclaim liberty to the captives, and the opening of the prison to those who are bound; to proclaim the acceptable year of the LORD, and the day of vengeance of our God; to comfort all who mourn.'*

James 4:7 *'Therefore submit to God. Resist the devil and he will flee from you.'*

Jeremiah 1:12 *'Then the LORD said to me, "You have seen well, for I am ready to perform My word."'*

John 10:10 *'The thief does not come except to steal, and to kill, and to destroy. I have come that they may have life, and that they may have it more abundantly.'*

John 11:18-19 *'Now Bethany was near Jerusalem, about two miles away. And many of the Jews had joined the women around Martha and Mary, to comfort them concerning their brother.'*

John 14:13 *'And whatever you ask in My name, that I will do, that the Father may be glorified in the Son.'*

John 14:9 *'Jesus said to him, "Have I been with you so long, and yet you have not known Me, Philip? He who has seen Me has seen the Father; so how can you say, 'Show us the Father?'*

John 15:7 *'If you abide in Me, and My words abide in you, you will ask what you desire, and it shall be done for you.'*

2 Corinthians 3:18 *'But we all, with unveiled face, beholding as in a mirror the glory of the Lord, are being transformed into the same image from glory to glory, just as by the Spirit of the Lord.'*

John 16:33 *'These things I have spoken to you, that in Me you may have peace. In the world you will have tribulation; but be of good cheer: I have overcome the world."*

Luke 4:18 *"The Spirit of the LORD is upon Me, Because He has anointed Me to preach the gospel to the poor; He has sent Me to heal the broken-hearted proclaim liberty to the captives and recovery of sight to the blind, to set at liberty those who are oppressed; to proclaim the acceptable year of the LORD."*

Luke 4:4 *'But Jesus answered him, saying, "It is written, 'Man shall not live by bread alone, but by every word of God."*

Luke 4:17-19 *'And He came down with them and stood on a level place with a crowd of His disciples and a great multitude of people from all Judea and Jerusalem, and from the seacoast of Tyre and Sidon, who came to hear Him and be healed of their diseases, as well as those who were tormented with unclean spirits; and they were healed. And the whole multitude sought to touch Him, for power went out from Him and healed them all.'*

Malachi 4:29 *'But to you who fear My name, the Sun of Righteousness shall arise with healing in His wings, and you shall go out and grow fat like stall-fed calves.'*

Mark 1:40-42 *'Now a leper came to Him, imploring Him, kneeling down to Him and saying to Him, "If You are willing, You can make me clean." Then Jesus, moved with compassion, stretched out His hand and touched him, and said to him, "I am willing; be cleansed." As soon as He had spoken, immediately the leprosy left him, and he was cleansed.'*

Mark 7:27 *'But Jesus said to her, "Let the children be filled first, for it is not good to take the children's bread and throw it to the little dogs."*

Matthew 12:34 *'For out of the abundance of the heart the mouth speaks.'*

Matthew 4:2 *'My son give attention to my words; incline your ear to my sayings. Keep them in the midst of your heart, for they are life to those who find then and healing to all their flesh.'*

Matthew 4:23 *'And Jesus went about all Galilee, teaching in their synagogues, preaching the gospel of the kingdom, and healing all kinds of sickness and all kinds of disease among the people.'*

Matthew 9:22 *'But Jesus turned around, and when He saw her, He said, "Be of good cheer, daughter; your faith has made you well." And the woman was made well from that hour.'*

Nahum 1:9 *'What do you conspire against the LORD? He will make an utter end of it. Affliction will not rise up a second time.'*

Numbers 6:24 *"The LORD bless you and keep you."*

Philippians 4:6-7 *'Be anxious for nothing, but in everything by prayer and supplication, with thanksgiving, let your requests be made known to God; and the peace of God, which surpasses all understanding, will guard your hearts and minds through Christ Jesus.'*

Philippians 2:10 *'That at the name of Jesus every knee should bow, of those in heaven, and of those on earth, and of those under the earth.'*

Philippians 2:13 *'For it is God who works in you both to will and to do for His good pleasure.'*

Philippians 4:8 *'Finally brethren, whatever things are true, whatever things are noble, whatever things are just, whatever things are pure, whatever things are lovely, whatever things are of good report, if there is any virtue and if there is anything praiseworthy — meditate on these things.'*

Proverbs 4:19-22 *'My son, give attention to my words; incline your ear to my sayings.do not let them depart from your eyes; keep them in the midst of your heart; for they are life to those who find them, and health to all their flesh.'*

Psalms 107:20 *'He sent His word and healed them and delivered them from their destructions.'*

Psalms 138:7 *'Though I walk in the midst of trouble, You will revive me; You will stretch out Your hand against the wrath of my enemies; and Your right hand will save me.'*

Psalm 1-3 *'Blessed is the man who walks not in the counsel of the ungodly, nor stands in the path of sinners, nor sits in the seat of the scornful; but his delight is in the law of the LORD, and in His law he meditates day and night. He shall be like a tree planted by the rivers of water, that brings forth its fruit in its season, whose leaf also shall not wither; and whatever he does shall prosper.'*

Psalm 103:1-5 *'Bless the LORD, O my soul and all that is within me, bless His holy name! Bless the LORD, O my soul, and forget not all His benefits; who forgives all your iniquities, who heals all your diseases, who redeems your life from destruction, who crowns you with lovingkindness and tender mercies, who satisfies your mouth with good things, so that your youth is renewed like the eagle's.'*

Psalm 112:7-8 *'He will not be afraid of evil tidings; his heart is steadfast, trusting in the LORD. His heart is established; he will not be afraid, until he sees his desire upon his enemies.'*

Psalm 118:17 *'I shall not die, but live, and declare the works of the LORD.'*

Psalm 125:3 *'For the sceptre of wickedness shall not rest on the land allotted to the righteous, Lest the righteous reach out their hands to iniquity.'*

Psalm 149:5-9 *'Let the saints be joyful in glory; let them sing aloud on their beds. Let the high praises of God be in their mouth, and a two-edged sword in their hand, to execute vengeance on the nations, and punishments on the peoples; to bind their kings with chains, and their nobles with fetters of iron; To execute on them the written judgment —* This honour have all His saints.'

Psalm 34:19 *'Many are the afflictions of the righteous, but the* L*ORD* *delivers him out of them all.'*

Psalm 89:34 *'My covenant I will not break, nor alter the word that has gone out of My lips.'*

Psalm 91:12-13 *'The righteous shall flourish like a palm tree, He shall grow like a cedar in Lebanon. Those who are planted in the house of the* L*ORD* *Shall flourish in the courts of our God. They shall still bear fruit in old age; They shall be fresh and flourishing, to declare that the* L*ORD* *is upright. He is my rock, and there is no unrighteousness in Him.'*

Romans 4:17 *'As it is written, "I have made you a father of many nations" in the presence of Him whom he believed God, who gives life to the dead and calls those things which do not exist as though they did.'*

Romans 5:17 *'For if by the one man's offence death reigned through the one, much more those who receive abundance of grace and of the gift of righteousness will reign in life through the One, Jesus Christ.'*

Romans 8:11 *'But if the Spirit of Him who raised Jesus from the dead dwells in you, He who raised Christ from the dead will also give life to your mortal bodies through His Spirit who dwells in you.'*

Romans 8:28 *'And we know that all things work together for good to those who love God, to those who are the called according to His purpose.'*

Romans 15:13 *'Now may the God of hope fill you with all joy and peace in believing, that you may abound in hope by the power of the Holy Spirit.'*

Zechariah 4:6 *'This is the word of the* Lord *to Zerubbabel: 'Not by might nor by power, but by My Spirit,' Says the* Lord *of hosts.'*

How to build a faith confession or declaration

For instance, if I were to use these twelve Scriptures…

1. Isaiah 53:4-5

2. John 3:16

3. Romans 4:20

4. Deuteronomy 28:61

5. Galatians 3:13

6. Hebrews 13:8

7. James 4:7

8. Matthew 4:24

9. Matthew 15:26

10. Matthew 21:19

11. 1 Corinthians 6:19

12. Romans 8:16

…I could put them together like this, to say:
'Lord, I thank you that you love me.'

'I thank you that healing belongs to me. I am your child and your word says that healing is the children's bread.'

'I thank you that you went to the cross for me, to bear my sicknesses and carry my diseases, so that I did not have to bear them. I believe that it is your will to heal me because It says in your Word that you healed all who came to you. Healing is available for me right now, because your Word says that you are the same yesterday today and forever.'

'So, today I am coming to you in the name of Jesus to receive by faith, the healing that you bought and paid for.'

'According to your Word, sickness is a curse that came because of disobedience to the law, but I am redeemed from every curse because you took the curse for me.'

'Lord, I understand that this sickness did not come from you, but that sickness is of the devil and the fallen world that we live in. As I have authority over the devil and sickness, I tell you satan to take your hands off my body and remove this sickness. I curse the root of it in Jesus name.'

'I thank you that your Holy Spirit lives in me and works the works of God.'

'I love you Lord. Thank you so much for healing me.' 'Amen.'

HELPFUL REFERENCES

You may find these books links to websites and references a help in your faith walk as I did There are so many which give a lot of good information in different areas…

Health

'Canceractive:' Chris Woollams; *'Credence:'* Philip Day; *'Eat Move Sleep'* by Tom Rath; *'The Rainbow Diet and how it can help you beat cancer.'* Chris Woollams; *'Rainbow Recipes,'* Chris Woollams and Barbara Cox.

Your general life

'The God Prescription,' by Dr Jackson; *'The Rainbow Diet and how it can help you beat cancer.'* Chris Woollams; *'Rainbow Recipes,'* Chris Woollams and Barbara Cox.

Mark Virkler also has many helpful blogs and articles about health on his website, www.cwgministries.org

Your spiritual diet

'The Healing of a Lady called Dodie Osteen,' by Dodie Osteen. There are many helpful videos on YouTube. Soak yourself in these positive messages. Here are a few examples; you could watch my own You Tube video, *'Margaret Cornell - Testimony';* Healing Scriptures, Kenneth Hagin. (and many other people); healing testimonies on YouTube from: *Andrew Wommack, Kenneth Copeland, Randy Clark. Bethel, CBN, 700 club.*

Ash Kotecha, The Healing Channel.

My Preached Testimony at Warminster: https://www.facebook.com/FCFWarminster/videos/239640780083109

Podcasts or YouTube sermons,

There are many ministers providing these messages on YouTube

e.g. *'Your words become your reality,'* by Joel Osteen;

'Casting your Cares upon the Lord,' by Kenneth Hagin;

'How to live and not die,' by Norvell Hayes;

'Receiving healing,' and *'God's will to heal!'* over 20 inspiring episodes by Keith Moore

Jentezen Franklin, https;//www.facebook.com/jentezenfranklin/videos/250369555619816/

'Laughter brings healing,' https://youtu.be/ GiogCaEXzgw

Audio book, T.L. Osbourne, '*Receive Miracle Healing*,' https://youtu.be/vq1XvIEoWtw

Kathryn Kuhlman, performing miracles through the Holy Spirit (and many more) https://youtu.be/JAiWgI6q5vc

Books:
Kynan Bridges, '*90 Days to Possessing Your Healing*,'

Charity Virkler Kayembe and Joe Brock, '*Everyday Angels*,'

Ali Loaker, '*Worship in the Storm.*' (This is the best book I've ever read about worship… tailor made for the time of trouble that you find yourself in!)

My own book '*A Life Shared*' available from my web site, Amazon or any bookshop